CW00734587

The Art *of* Picnics

ALANNA O'NEIL

The Art *of* Picnics

SEASONAL OUTDOOR ENTERTAINING

yellow pear press

CORAL GABLES

For permission requests, please contact the publisher at:
Mango Publishing Group
2850 S Douglas Road, 2nd Floor
Coral Gables, FL 33134 USA
info@mango.bz

For special orders, quantity sales, course adoptions and corporate sales, please email the publisher at sales@mango.bz. For trade and wholesale sales, please contact Ingram Publisher Services at customer.service@ingramcontent.com or +1.800.509.4887.

The Art of Picnics: Seasonal Outdoor Entertaining

Library of Congress Cataloging-in-Publication number: 2021938421
ISBN: (print) 978-1-64250-646-4, (ebook) 978-1-64250-647-1
BISAC category code: CKB060000, COOKING / Methods / Outdoor

Printed in the United States of America

"LIVE IN EACH SEASON AS IT PASSES; BREATHE THE AIR, DRINK THE DRINK, TASTE THE FRUIT, AND RESIGN YOURSELF TO THE INFLUENCE OF THE EARTH."

—HENRY DAVID THOREAU

CONTENTS

PREFACE

It wouldn't be true to say that this book happened entirely as a career pivot a few years ago. The idea of this book had been nagging at me for quite some time. At a time of uncertainty and change in my life, I finally took a hard look at what I had quietly hushed away in the back of my mind. In a world where we're craving connection to each other and nature, I felt like it was the appropriate time to put the pen to paper, so to speak. My journey from growing up on a small rural farm in Vermont, to living in the hustle of New York City, to finding balance in Hawaii has been the foundation for this book. The concept evolved into something more than simply home cooking and entertaining.

We find ourselves in an ever-changing, fast-paced society in which often lose sight of the present moment that quietly passes by with the multitude of distractions. On a deeper level, I feel like we have a blurred vision of what it truly means to connect with one another and ourselves. We all acknowledge the power of disconnecting to reconnect, but how often does this happen in reality? Moreover, do we make it a priority to set time aside to share a sunset or pause to hear the chorus of songbirds awaken with the sun over hot coffee? It's these types of moments that seem far and few between. Making time to be present for each other and ourselves in the solace and wonder that is nature is immensely healing and restorative. It really is the little things that make lasting memories. The seeds of this book were planted in my childhood and came to realization with my new life in Hawaii. They have become the underlying thread woven throughout, as I hope you will see.

Everyone has had unique, impressionable experiences in childhood that shaped how we see ourselves today. No childhood is exactly the same even if you live under the same roof. Perhaps I've become more reflective in my thirties, but I realized how deeply our experiences and perceptions shape our core beliefs. Growing up on a horse farm in rural Vermont was incredibly idyllic and peaceful. It was a childhood spent having tea parties in my mother's garden and playing in the pine woods, which my siblings and I appropriately called the "Secret Forest." With the arrival and passing of every season, there was something new to celebrate. Whether it was picking the heavily laden apple trees in the orchard during the fall or the resplendent peonies in the spring, we were taught to cherish every seasonal blessing. My childhood revolved around the seasons in such a rhythm that I haven't fully felt since. With such vast grounds for us to play and explore in, every day held a new adventure in our little world.

Our home itself was a thing to behold when I was a young girl. My mother is an artist and wedding florist and grew most of the flowers for her weddings. The gardens were not perfect despite the painstaking work of maintaining them, but they were always in bloom and bountiful. We lived within our means and my mother always did her best to make any gathering lovely and special with what she had on hand. My parents are the sort who appreciate antiquity and things of the past and our home reflected that sentimentality. Our childhood was even more naive without television or other modern comforts. We were left to our own imagination and nature to occupy ourselves. My mother was just as creative as we were to keep us out of trouble and boredom.

No matter the weather or season, my mother would usher us out the door for a family outing. Vermont can be quite bleak in the winter, not to mention a frozen like tundra with arctic cold winds. With six (yes, six) seasons, the weather was always the talk of conversation. It could be a gorgeous warm blue day and nearly below freezing the next with a chance of snow. The fickle New England weather can be quite difficult to plan around. Nevertheless, my mother would make it a point to organize an outing with some family friends, regardless of the weather. You can be sure if there was a sunny day in the forecast, the whole neighborhood would be frolicking outside. In her resourceful multitasking way, she would pack up sandwiches, treats, and the like to rally us all outside. Whether it was in the heart of winter or a lazy day spent by the pond, she always managed to put something together to bring along and share. All our little family picnics were simple, using what we had and what was growing in the garden. The seasons even more so inspired what we could rustle up from the pantry and where to go explore. Everyone had its own traditions and annual activities that even the smallest among us took note of what the season had in store. We rightly called out if any were to be missed, especially it if involved mud, snow, or sand. There was always something to look forward to with every passing month, each unique.

It was these seasonal family moments that I will never forget. They have shaped how I see the world and how there is so much beauty in simplicity in the little things. I owe my appreciation for nature and food to my mother. As an artist, she instilled in me to ability to see the beauty in all things even as mundane as a fallen tree. Picnicking was simply a way she showed us how to appreciate the natural beauty around us, be resourceful, and how to be present with those we love. These memories have inspired me to create this collection of recipes and stories. They convey a sense of place, belonging, and warmth with a familiarity of sharing a beautiful meal outside.

The book is divided into four seasons with unique menus for each that I hope entice you to head outside. They are centered around seasonal activities with complementary stories. The recipes are family favorites, some old and some new, that can be easily adapted to your own taste and what you have on hand. You will find that the majority of these recipes can be prepared beforehand. Share the recipes with your family and friends so that everyone can contribute to a wholesome and fun outing.

I hope you find inspiration to gather with those you love in the great outdoors, celebrating life's simple joys.

PREPARE & GATHER

With a little thought and care beforehand, a simple gathering can be transformed into an exceptional and memorable outing. When you have a set date and your fingers are crossed for good weather, thinking ahead of what you can prepare will much easier, even in the smallest ways. After all, headaches, stress, and frustration should be left at home or at the office. An intimate family outing to your local beach should be fun, casual, and easy. Anything else defeats the whole purpose entirely! For a larger potluck picnic, organize as much as you can beforehand and don't hesitate to delegate if need be. If you can wrangle up some help from a friend or neighbor, all the better. Leaving the work for yourself is simply not enjoyable (unless you are that elusive type of person) and you certainly will be exhausted at the end of it. After all, picnics are about sharing and that includes the cooking and packing. Even on a small family outing, everyone pitching in to help makes the day more relaxing and smoother. My mother's rule of thumb was that if we wanted to go camp out by the lake, we had to help; it was that simple.

The weather is the elephant in the room when it comes to planning a picnic, especially for one that requires a trek or drive. Regardless, always have a backup plan and if that means the backyard or next weekend, so be it. If you can make the call the day before, let all your friends and family know so they can plan accordingly. Despite how much you may have prepared already, reality and practicality win at the end of the day. If you've got the green light, gather up the cooler, linens, serveware, blankets and any other bits you will need the night before. This can be a great task for the little ones who love to feel helpful and want to contribute in some way. While my mother cooked or baked, she would give each of us duties such as to pack the silverware or choose what flowers to bring. We felt like the lucky one if we had the grand responsibility of choosing the color of the napkins. If it happens to be a spontaneous idea, pack the essentials and leave the fancy details behind. What matters most is simply heading out the door. I've often found that it's those last, spur-of-the-moment ones that truly are special, especially if the weather is glorious.

Waking up to a bright winter day can stir anyone with cabin fever to venture out in the cold. Vermont is one of the cloudiest states in the country and, if we have a bold blue day, you can be sure everyone is outside, even in the winter months. Practicality and patience are even important to consider, especially with any little ones. When everyone can't seem to find their matching mitten or is taking ages to don their many layers, a patient sigh is guaranteed to be heard. I remember my mother once shoveled off the pond for us, which is no easy task, mind you, to play hockey. We were eager to help but probably made more work for her in the end.

We had lanterns set surrounding the entire pond around dusk. We were taking ages to get ready, but she the queen of multitasking helped us, while her entire sausage roast and homemade buns burned to a crisp in the fire, but we made the best of our very barbecued picnic. The pure joy of skating around each other in circles under the stars with lanterns was a moment to cherish. No matter what a scenario or season may bring, always be up for an adventure. Practicality, patience, and an easy-going attitude should be packed up right next to the sandwiches.

Transporters

Not every basket is created equally, and some are quite impractical. When shopping for a basket, consider the construction and handles primarily. The handles should be heavy duty and reinforced. The small, flimsy baskets you often see are just for decoration. Look for a high-quality European-style market tote; they are often higher priced but will live to tell the tales of many outings. Canvas totes are attractive and practical, too, as they are washable. It is trickier to find a quality wooden basket these days; often the metal bits break on the handles. If you do find one, be sure it's reinforced on the bottom and able to carry several pounds. Sometimes, they aren't the most realistic option as they can be a bit cumbersome to carry when heavy compared to a sturdy tote. Traditional wicker hampers are also an ideal all-around option to consider since they often come complete with serving utensils, glasses, and plates. Additionally, the flat sides can be transformed into a makeshift cutting surface, too. For breakable items such as ceramic dishes, vases, or other fragile items, I prefer to use wooden crates. You can wrap the fragile items with tea towels and nestle them together for protection.

Coolers can carry a heavy load, and I prefer to use them for a larger picnic or on a whole day out. Although they are not as attractive as baskets, wheeled coolers are back-savers. They also can be a makeshift cutting board or assembly surface. Consider having at least two sizes, a smaller hand-held one and a larger wheeled option. Galvanized pails or buckets also make great porters and can double as ice bucket for beverages.

If you have a longer trek, consider pulling out the old red wagon or cart to haul your goods. It's worth investing in a good one to save many trips to the car. They are especially helpful when you don't have a few extra hands to help carry heavy items (or carry a tired little one). A trusty old backpack will never fail on a hike or picnic in the woods. On a snowy day, a sled or toboggan is essential.

Serveware

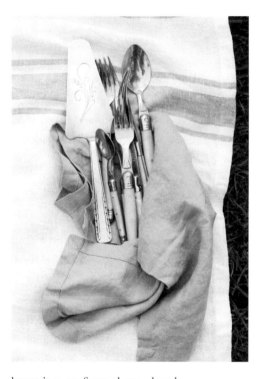

Unlike the Victorians who set out to impress with their fine china and dinnerware, modern picnic goers can be more practical. Consider using enamelware as it is light, highly durable, and most importantly, eco-friendly. There are some sets and designs that look like porcelain or ceramic, too. Keep a lookout at flea markets or estate sales for vintage enamelware, you may find some gems to treasure. You can often find tumblers in the same enamelware set, but there are great options out there for unbreakable acrylic cups and wine glasses. Etsy is a treasure trove of vintage finds. Picking up a few mix-and-matched plates that you don't mind the getting the odd chip or broken is a pretty and affordable way to take it up a notch. And of course, leaving your ceramic dishes at home keeps it away from clumsy hands.

Lastly, a brief but important note on one-time use utensils and serveware: It is common knowledge that plastic is wasteful and harmful to our environment, ocean, and wildlife, especially little bits such as cutlery. It's disheartening to see nature sprinkled with trash and plastic, and it certainly detracts from an otherwise ideal picnic spot. With widely (and more attractive) alternatives like enamel, bamboo, or melamine readily available, reusable (rather than disposable) serveware is the obvious choice in my eyes and necessary for our precious planet. A conscious choice that as my mother would say, is the right thing to do.

Linens & Blankets

Like your wardrobe, spending a little more on quality items that are made to last is worthwhile in the long run. Investing in good cloth napkins make that extra special difference. I prefer to use linen as they not only wear and wash well but soften with age. They also don't need to look perfectly tidy or ironed if you take them straight out of the dryer. Choose a neutral-colored set or an accent color that coordinates with your reusable dish set. For napkin patterns, I prefer small neutral stripes or a neutral floral design. Soft blues, grays, blush, creams, and warm beiges are some of my favorite color options.

When it comes time to lay out your spread, a fancy picnic blanket isn't necessary. Your dining tablecloths that are little more worn can work nicely for a family day out. There are some wool blankets that are machine washable which are great options for cooler days. Old quilts and oversized beach blankets also fit the bill. Ideally aim for anything that is washable, light, and easy to pack. Opt out of any whites or creams unless you can live knowing they may get a little chocolate handprint or muddy paws prints on them.

For a special occasion (and if it's practical), I love to include lightweight flat woven rugs or bring a small table. It adds some height and creates a lounge-like feel. The wooden crates used to transport the goods can be flipped and disguised with a napkin. Be sure to set up on level ground if you decide to add a small table with the rug, otherwise, many parks have picnic tables and benches that can be easily spruced up with the right details.

Cutting Boards

Having a good selection of cutting boards to choose from will make organizing and setting up your picnic much easier. Try and have a variety of sizes for different types of food such as appetizers and desserts. The light, narrow, and longer boards are in frequent rotation for me. It is also helpful to bring a small cutting board that is specifically for assembling or cutting, especially if you are grilling. Although I prefer wood, they can become quite heavy, but there are lighter alternatives like bamboo. Platters, trays, and low-profile baskets lined with a linen napkin also serve as attractive and lighter alternatives to a wood serving board.

Storage

Most picnics include leftovers, so encourage your guests bring their own storage containers so they can bring home the extra abundance and continue to share in the bounty. Generally, it's best to save the original wrappings and packaging so they can be reused. I also like to tuck in a few extra reusable storage bags just in case. Glass, tin, enamel, or Bee's Wrap® are eco-friendly options. Everyone has a few Mason jars around the house, and they are durable options for both storing and transporting. Thermoses, stoppered bottles, and steel bottles are ideal for hot and cold beverages alike. You can get creative with storing liquids and transfer them into something prettier such as an enamel pitcher once you reach your picnic location.

Kitchen and Food Accoutrements

One beautiful reason to share a delicious meal outside is to celebrate the natural beauty surrounding you. Since the convenience of your kitchen may be far away, I find it helpful to prepare a supply bag with other food accoutrements and tools. A Mason jar of extra virgin olive oil, lemons, salt, pepper, and mustard are just a few to include. A few kitchen tools that may come in handy are scissors, a small bowl, wine opener, paring knife, and can opener. Put together a little kit with these essentials based on the dishes you're bringing to make packing easier. Better to be over prepared than unable to open up that wine bottle!

Disposal

Our family motto was to leave a place better than we found it. Even if there were some wrappers or bits of plastic floating around from previous hikers, we were encouraged to collect them along with our own before we headed home. Aim to leave your special spot cleaner than when you arrived, not only for others but out of respect for nature and the other fuzzy and feathered inhabitants. Bring along a large garbage bag or two for your waste. If there isn't a bin close by, you can dispose of it at home.

Little Extra Somethings

Apart from a gorgeous backdrop or tranquil landscape, adding thoughtful details when you can will elevate your gathering to something quite special. For extra comfort, I like to lay out a few pillows for seating. Sometimes the decorative ones pulled straight from the couch or spare room work perfectly. Ones that are oversized, neutral in color, and with a removable cover pass the pillow test for me. Of course, including them is not always realistic, but for intimate occasions or when it suits your location, they make lounging under the backyard tree all the more comfortable. Just beware of those grass stains! The flat floor pillows or even the cushions from your dining room chairs pair well with a low-profile table. Pillows are like the cherry on top; they make your picnic feel all the more inviting. The little ones will love them, too, but maybe forgo the whites just to be safe.

Greenery & Flowers

A spring or summer picnic is not complete without some colorful and seasonal blooms. Flowers may seem a bit extravagant for your average outing, but they add a thoughtful touch. My mother, being a wedding florist, always added her floral flourish from the gardens to every family get-together. I try to use seasonal flowers whenever I can if I have any growing in the garden. A simple and fresh bouquet of wildflowers picked on the roadside is just as lovely as a store-bought arrangement. Personally, I like the thoughtfulness of gathering your own or arranging some local beauties from the farmers market yourself.

Get creative with any wild greenery that you may come upon. Maui is blessed with an abundance of wild and tropical greens at every corner. I bet your neighborhood is, too, if you look closely. Olive branches are one of my favorites to adorn rustic dishes and cheeseboards as they hold up well without water and are simply elegant. Pine boughs, eucalyptus, ferns, citrus leaves, ivy, morning glory vines, and nasturtiums are just a few others to name that you may come across on your hunt. Although anything from the backyard will do just fine!

For display, I like to use a sturdy enamel or ceramic pitcher for stability rather than a slim vase. Another sweet idea is scattering little bud vases with a single blossom on your serving trays or table. I love to use fresh herbs, too, where I can. Tuck in a few sprigs around the cheese board or in your bouquet. Rosemary and thyme especially add a rustic homegrown touch, not to mention a pleasant fragrance. Herbs are an inexpensive way to dress up any table or dish. Fresh seasonings right at your fingertips.

The Vermont foliage season in autumn is one of those absolutely stunning times of the year that flashes by in an instant like the season's fiery and golden hues. Even if you have lived in New England your entire life, it truly does not get old year after year. Peak season lasts about a week or so when the trees are aflame before losing their precious leaves. It also marks the harvest with an overwhelming bounty from the garden. For an autumnal themed gathering, incorporate gourds, pumpkins, or squashes alongside your dishes. Branches with vibrant leaves, sunflowers, or corn husks can be arranged together for a festive accent. This season's palette has the most striking of colors to use for inspiration in your garnishes.

For those in colder climates, winter months can prove to be a bit of a challenge to find fresh flowers. It takes just a little more creativity to embellish your spread. Although you'll be surprised by how a few fresh pine boughs and wild winter berries from the woods can create a bright and magical arrangement. Cranberries and citrus fruits are another colorful option to liven up your winter spreads. Halve oranges and juicy grapefruits and nestle them alongside your dishes or boards. Think festive berries, cedar, holly, and all those wintery greens. It is possible to have some fun outside in the middle of winter—it just will take a little extra work and maybe a few glasses of mulled wine.

Lighting

Depending on the season or time of day you venture out, adding a few candles or lanterns can tastefully enhance your scene. Sprinkling tea light candles around your picnic spread is an enchanting way to create an intimate and cozy feel. (If you are picnicking someplace with dry foliage, be sure the candles are battery operated, rather than flame candles! Starting a fire would not be a good way to end your outing!) To really create something ethereal, light a few lanterns that encircle your picnic for a welcoming atmosphere. Galvanized metal and other decorative lanterns are easy ways to refine a backyard picnic or one close to home. If you are in a location that is safe for open flames, scatter a few citronella candles around the perimeter of your feast to ward off those pesky and persistent mosquitos in the summer months. They are the ultimate uninvited guests, indeed. Flameless candles also are great and safer alternatives if you have little ones running about or, like me, a wild puppy!

An Eye on the Sky

While the idea of heading out on a picnic with the family may sound like a wonderful idea to occupy the kids on a Saturday afternoon, the importance of checking the weather beforehand can't be underestimated. Any significant rain and wind in the forecast are serious factors to consider if you are planning ahead. Have umbrellas and anoraks handy if there is a slight a chance of rain. Reusable fabric food covers are also a great investment that tents your feast and protects from sand, blowing leaves, dirt, and those pesky, persistent ants. Outdoor canopy tents can be a savior if rain may show up as the unwelcome guest.

Picnic Ready

For easy packing, create a small picnic bag at the ready so you don't have to think twice when you fancy an outdoor outing. Here are some suggestions that can be gathered and set aside beforehand that will be ready for a whim or when the weather calls. Collect and store these essential items into a tote bag or basket.

Linen napkins   *Tea towel*
Enamel plates   *Disposable wipes*
Glassware   *Bug spray*
Picnic blanket   *Storage bags*
Opinel knife   *Garbage bag*
Chef's knife   *Scissors*
A set of utensils   *First aid kit*
Serving utensils
Jar of extra virgin olive oil
Wine opener
Salt and pepper shakers
Small cutting board

POP UP & PANTRY PICNICS

The idea of dusting off the old basket in the cellar and creating an elaborate spread to schlep up a mountain can seem a bit overwhelming and unreasonable. It certainly does to me sometimes when I've had a long day and the general idea of packing and unpacking is the last thing I want to do. I'll be honest by saying that having a sit down to watch the sunset does take a little more effort than sitting down at the table. Although, packing a picnic is not so much about shopping all day for ingredients and prepping the whole day to me anyway, but rather being resourceful and creative with what I have on hand. As a little girl, when I declared from the open fridge there was nothing to bring for our planned hike, we would rummage around in the pantry and fridge using up any odd bits here and there, and before you know it, there was a feast to behold. You will find that many of these recipes, though they're seasonal, are open to you using what you have already. Having a well-stocked pantry is just the place to start. Plus, it gives you a nudge of motivation to follow that spontaneous idea to holler to your friends or kids in the other room, "We're going on a picnic." Although not every outing needs to be thoroughly planned with all the frills and fuss, a few delicious provisions, homemade or not, wrapped up in backpack for an impromptu picnic in the park is equally wonderful. I find that something more relaxed and casual is far more enjoyable than an outing that is highly embellished and meticulously planned.

The start of every great picnic, in my mind, comes from taking a good look and inventory of your pantry and fridge. I remember once my mother opened the pantry doors, making a grand gesture and saying aloud, "Well, let's see what we have here to work with," as she visually took stock. Perhaps there are some leftovers that can be transformed with a little cooking magic into an entirely different dish all together or odds and ends of cheese, meats, and olives that can pass as a well thought out cheese board. The idea of spending a fortune on a picnic meal simply doesn't suit my lifestyle nor budget, frankly. And I find that it takes away from the whole idea and meaning behind it altogether.

Of course, it does require a stop to the store, but I can pretty much guarantee that you have the makings of a lovely little feast in the pantry and fridge already. Not only is a well-stocked pantry a happy marriage for your picnic basket, but it saves you time from many trips to the store and will supply goodies for an impromptu outing.

Here are a few things to consider to make your pantry and fridge picnic ready.

First things first, take stock of what you have. Having a plentiful supply of grains, crackers, pasta, and rice that are staples for many picnic dishes will come in handy. If you are a baker like me, flour, sugar, maple syrup (essential, in my book), honey, nuts, and the rest of a baker's loot is ideal, especially when you are in the mood to whip up a batch of cookies to bring along. You'd be surprised how a homely box of oats and chocolate chips combined together can be all the encouragement needed to pack up the bags. On the savory end, olives, roasted red peppers, canned tomatoes, artichoke hearts, canned beans, whole grain mustard, and other spreads make the idea of picnicking a little more convenient.

Pantry Essentials

Pasta in any shape, especially smaller ones such as penne, rotelle, fusilli, orecchiette, and farfalle.

A variety of grains such as bulgur, farro, barley, quinoa, and brown rice are sure to be on my shelf.

Canned preserves such as pickles (pickled anything, really), roasted red peppers, artichoke hearts, mustards, jams, olive oil packed tuna, hot sauce, capers, tapenade, and olives, of course, top my list.

Legumes, canned or otherwise, such as beans, chickpeas, and lentils will come out shining for you one day.

Extra virgin olive oil is a staple for me. Also, a good selection of nut oils, vinegars, and tahini will do wonders for a basic salad.

Having few varieties of crackers at the ready can't be forgotten. Nor other crunchy bits like salted almonds, pecans, walnuts, and other nuts and seeds.

Baking staples such as flour, old-fashioned oats, baking soda, baking powder, spices, sugar, dark chocolate, pure vanilla extract, dried fruit, maple syrup, and honey are essential for a home baker.

Although the greens and fresh fruit and veggies in the fridge changes week to week, there are a few items that I do always have on standby.

Produce

Lemons

Broccoli rabe

Radicchio

Garlic

Shallots

Onions of any kind

Arugula

Swiss chard

Tuscan kale

Tomatoes

Fresh berries of any kind

Red grapes

Apples

Avocados

Fresh herbs such as basil, thyme, sage, rosemary, parsley, cilantro, mint, dill, and oregano

Perishable Provisions

Milk or nut milk if you prefer

A good butter, both unsalted and salted

Cream cheese or mascarpone

Hummus or your favorite dip

A dozen or two eggs

A sandwich style bread for slicing

A rustic sourdough loaf

A small assortment of cheeses such as Parmigiano-Reggiano, sharp cheddar,
Pecorino Romano, fresh mozzarella, chèvre, and a feta; stock up on your top picks

One or two cured meats or cold cuts

Apart from pantry and fresh produce staples, there are a few more vital ingredients I always have on hand. A parting pantry thought: a well-stocked pantry is well provisioned.

Pop Up Picnics: A Note on the Office Lunch Hour

With a picnic-ready pantry, you'll find putting together a quick picnic is a lot simpler than it may seem. And on that note, your lunch time at the office just got a lot more interesting and healthier. While I was living in the city (and by city, I mean New York), I desperately tried to make any excuse to take lunch out to the nearest park, which happened to be Bryant Park, right in the heart of the fashion district. It has to be said that while most of my colleges ate in front of their computer, it did seem odd at the time (to them, anyway) that I went out. The park was mostly in shadow due to the towering buildings that surround this precious little green gem tucked away among the fabric stores and offices, but this was my daily escape. I typically packed my own lunch or picked up a few things here and there along the way before settling into an empty chair as far away from the crowds as I could find. Not only was I physically hungry from the stress of working in high fashion, but mentally and spiritually hungry, as sentimental as that may sound. I relished in the relative peace under the green canopy, apart from the broken record of the New York soundtrack of taxis and sirens. Simply taking a moment to get some fresh air with a homely yet delicious packed lunch of a ham sandwich slathered with mustard and cold grapes left me satiated in more ways than one. Herein lies one point about having a well-stocked pantry. Whether you work in an office or for yourself, taking lunch outside on to the nearest park with your coworkers or just yourself won't seem so out of the ordinary. Perhaps everyone can bring a little something from home or picked up at the corner store for a one-hour lunch time feast. I think we can all agree that eating in front of a computer screen is not healthy for your body, mind, and spirit. Whether it's thirty minutes or an hour out, you will come back with a clear head, smile, and all the more prepared to handle the rest of your workday, and dare I say even more productive!

SEASONAL SPREADS

One of the most delightful sights to see is a gorgeous and plentiful cheese board. It literally is a feast for the eyes with layers of crisp crackers, overflowing nuts, and slabs of creamy cheese. A thoughtful board is a true celebration of the sweet and savory that does not need to cost a fortune. A simple board with fresh fruit and a wedge of cheese nestled between two lovers in a private spot under the shelter of a tree has been painted by artists throughout the centuries. Besides the works of Manet or Renoir, literature, too, has romanticized the glories of a delicious spread like the generous hodge-podge of Rat's picnic in my all-time favorite classic, *The Wind in the Willows* by Kenneth Grahame. As old as the leisurely activity is, it is nowhere near out of style. It is a picnic in a pinch if you have limited time, but still heartily satisfying. Crafting a deliciously curated grazing board takes a little forethought but knowing these few key elements will help guide you while you plan out your little feast.

A Cheese Trio

When shopping around your local cheese shop or store, think of this holy trinity of cheese, if you will: sheep, cow, and goat. These are based on the types of milk, of course, from each that rounds out a nicely balanced board. Pick up one of each to have a distinct variety and taste, at least a quarter pound of each per person.

Another thought to consider is color and texture. Aim to select a variety between soft, creamy, semi-firm, and firm, craggy extra aged cheeses. The rich cheese palette ranges from pure white, pale gold, ochre, and even a deep blue or red such as inky blue Roquefort or a cranberry studded Wensleydale. Be sure to include a few different hues and textures for an interesting and visually appealing platter.

Don't hesitate to ask your local cheese purveyor or monger behind the counter to steer you in the right direction. They are very knowledgeable, and I can guarantee would love to chit chat on their expertise about some of their new finds or perhaps suggest something you never considered trying before. Striking up a conversation with them about your picnic plans will not only leave them feeling useful but may leave you a few extra wedges gifted in with a wink.

Here are a few of my favorites to get you started:

Jasper Hill's Cabot Cloth Bound Cheddar
Vermont Creamery Goat Cheese
Extra aged Manchego
Brie
Stilton
Quality aged Parmigiano-Reggiano
Saint Marcellin
Cranberry Wensleydale
Gruyère
Camembert

Charcuterie

To partner with your cheeses, including an assortment of charcuterie rounds out a savory board, in my opinion. Opt for one type of salami, the classic saucisson-sec, chorizo, and finocchiona, though these are just a few to name. There are a wide variety of options, normally crafted with herbs, seasonings, or even wine. Choose your favorite or pick one that sounds delicious and give it a go.

Cured meats also make delectable accompaniments to your board. Prosciutto, capicola, and soppressata are my preferred picks. Consider a quarter pound per person as a rough rule of thumb. If you have the palate (which I don't despite my year living abroad in Paris) include a forcemeat such as a pâté, mousse, or terrine. They are exceptionally rich and definitely add that elusive element of the French sophistication I have yet to master. You'll be feasting by the Seine in no time.

Garden Gems

With all the richness from the cheese and meats, having a selection of something crisp, bright, and fresh is essential. I look no further than the garden to see what I can rustle up to include for vegetables and fruit. Of course, there is the classic yet staple crisp bunch of grapes which undoubtedly will always be included. Although, I like to serve what is seasonal and creative when it comes to vegetables and fruit. A seasonal offering by far out wins a basic crudité platter, in my book. Those carrots and radishes patiently waiting to be plucked in the garden can be washed and peeled, left with a little bit of the green leafy top for an easy pick up. The cherry tomatoes that are dripping in puddles to the ground can be piled on like gemstones. Lest we forget, the forever abundant cucumber that leaves us at the end of the season wondering what to do with them all. Picking straight from the garden or stopping at your local's farmers market is by far more rewarding and wholesome than the plastic-wrapped baby carrots. The farmers market is a perfect place to shop for all of your picnic needs. A one-stop shop for fresh produce, flowers, baked goods…all ripe and ready for you. Choosing what is season locally is not only healthier but more thoughtful and resourceful as well. Every season has its vibrant and abundant harvest, even winter. Mindfully select two or three seasonal fruits and vegetables for a well-balanced and hearty spread.

One other bit of greenery I like to include on all my boards is fresh herbs from the garden. Whether it's rosemary, thyme, sage, or basil, tucked in or nestled herbs around a block of cheese is fragrant and simply pretty.

Spring

Raw snap peas	*Cauliflower*
Raw sugar peas	*Radishes*
Blanched asparagus	*Tangerines*
Roasted artichokes	*Grapefruit*
Belgian endive	*Lilikoi (passion fruit)*

Summer

Cherry tomatoes	*Figs*	*Pineapple*
Heirloom tomatoes slices	*Cherries*	*Peaches*
Rainbow carrots	*Berries of any kind*	*Nectarines*
Broccoli florets	*Watermelon*	*Anything growing in the garden!*
Cucumber spears	*Papaya*	
Blanched green beans	*Melon*	

Autumn

Persimmons

Pomegranate

Apples

Pears

Cranberries

Grapes

Beets

Rainbow carrots

Winter

Pickles (anything pickled from the summer)	Roasted Brussels sprouts
Dried fruit	Chestnuts
Fennel	Roasted carrots
Oranges (citrus fruit)	Roasted red pepper
Olives	Roasted garlic

You can, of course, mix and match between every season as most of these are widely available year-round, but I like to stay as seasonal as I can with what is local and picked right from the tree or dirt!

Bread & Crackers

Bread, crackers, and other crispy bits will be a foundation for all that gooey cheese and salty salami. I would be a very happy camper with just a good bread, cheese, and salami. Like the rest of your board offerings, buy the best you can find or afford. A good baguette either toasted for crostini with garlic and olive oil or simply plain is just perfect. Crispy farmhouse crackers, pita, flatbreads, and focaccia will be crowd-pleasers for sure. Similar to selecting cheese, I like to offer at least two different textures, one softer option like a ciabatta, and a crisper, crunchier alternative like a seeded cracker. Toasting up tortillas or even sandwich wraps can be broken up into shards which are delicious, too. Although, a homemade loaf on the counter certainly won't disappoint, either.

Other Sweet and Savory Bits

Now to finish it off, there several other bits I like to include that complement any board. These spreads and crunchy additions can be tucked in and around the board in smaller serving bowls.

Grainy mustard

Fig preserves

Jam or a fruit curd

Dark chocolate pieces

Relish

Nuts, either salted or raw

Wildflower honey

Hummus

Dolmas

Olive tapenade

Pesto

Pickles

Cornichons

With such a curated board for a special picnic, why not dress it up a bit? Again, I look to the season for inspiration to add some festive and pretty trimmings. One easy trick that takes little effort and adds a pop of color is nestling in halved citrus fruit around the board. Tangerines and blood oranges are bursts of color to what could be an otherwise neutral board of cheese and crackers. Edible flower heads graciously plucked from the garden are stunning, too. Adding little touches like these will make all the difference to share a thoughtful presentation, especially for a celebratory gathering. Of course, it may not be realistic for a day in the park with the kids, but when the moment arises to impress or a special occasion for two, consider adding a few extra trimmings. Bring your clippers and forage around the garden, backyard, or on your drive home. I like to keep a pair in my glove compartment. You're bound to find something beautiful right under your nose. With whatever beautiful bits you find, be sure that the greenery and flowers are nontoxic. This is meant to be the fun part, not a hassle to find or put you out of your budget—effortless natural details when it's practical for you.

Seasonal Trimmings

Spring

Tulips
Primroses
Cornflowers
Nasturtiums
Mint
Sunflower sprouts
Chives
Dill
Parsley

Summer

Roses
Dahlias
Lavender
Hibiscus
Honeysuckle
Olive branches
Basil
Cilantro
Tomato vines

Spring

Dried maple leaves
Wheat
Mini gourds and pumpkins
Honeycomb
Thyme
Rosemary
Sage
Bay leaves

Winter

Pine tree clippings
Holly
Wild winter berries
Cedar
Juniper
Oregano
Acorns
Rose hips
Pinecones

Once you've gathered your goodies and natural trimmings, find a solid and sturdy cutting board or platter as your blank canvas. Ideally, it should be light enough to carry but large enough to hold your delicious provisions. Wood, naturally, is my material of choice; it's rustic and practical rather than stone or slate which could break along the way. Store any trimmings you've found in the cooler, if necessary, with any meats, fruits, and vegetables. Cheeses, on the other hand, especially softer ones, can do with an hour or so out at room temperature. Bringing them to room temperature allows them to breathe and open up like wine. They can be wrapped up and stored in your basket unless it is an extremely hot day or a longer trek. That being said, don't forget the cheese knives!

ROASTED GRAPE & ROSEMARY FOCACCIA

Serves 4-6

2 ¼ teaspoons active dry yeast

1 ¾ cup water

1 teaspoon wildflower honey

3 ½ cups bread flour

3 tablespoons extra virgin olive oil

1 teaspoon kosher salt

½ cup cornmeal

½ cup red seedless grapes
   (concord or ruby)

2 garlic cloves, minced

½ cup red onions, thinly sliced

1 tablespoon fresh rosemary

1 teaspoon Italian seasoning

¼ cup Pecorino Romano, grated

¼ cup Parmigiano-Reggiano, grated

Maldon salt

Optional:

½ pound prosciutto de Parma

1 cup baby arugula

Although you can't go wrong with a good crusty baguette, this focaccia takes it up a notch, making it a perfect addition to any picnic, frankly. When roasted, the grapes burst with a toasty sweetness in your mouth that is the right match for the savory herbs and cheese. You can cut it up into bite-size squares and serve it as an appetizer, too. For something more substantial, top it with prosciutto and arugula when you reach your picnic site for utmost freshness.

Using a stand mixer with a dough hook, combine the yeast, water, and honey into the mixing bowl. Using a spoon, stir together until the yeast is dissolved.

Add the flour and 2 tablespoons of olive oil. Knead for about 5 minutes on medium speed, scraping the down sides of the bowl if necessary. Let the dough rest for fifteen minutes.

Add in the salt and knead for another 8 minutes on medium speed.

Remove the dough from the mixing bowl and place into another lightly greased bowl with olive oil and cover with plastic wrap. Let it rise for 2 hours in a warm spot.

Preheat the oven to 425°F.

Once the dough is at least doubled in size, lightly grease a fifteen-by-twelve-inch rimmed baking sheet with evenly coated with tablespoon of olive oil. Sprinkle the cornmeal on the tray.

The dough will be very wet, unlike a regular pizza dough. Pour out the dough onto the tray, patting it down to every corner as best as you can. Continue to pat down the dough; it should just about fill the tray.

Let the dough rise for another 30 minutes in a warm place.

Once the dough has rested, drizzle a tablespoon of olive oil over the dough. It will be puffier and soft to the touch.

Scatter the grapes (cut them in half if very large), garlic, and red onions evenly over the dough. Continue to sprinkle the rosemary and Italian seasoning. Finish it off by sprinkling on the Pecorino Romano and Parmigiano-Reggiano.

Bake for about 15 to 20 minutes until the edges and bottom are golden brown.

Once baked, sprinkle a pinch of Maldon salt over the focaccia. Let it cool before serving.

When you are ready to serve, top the focaccia with the optional prosciutto and arugula. For easier packing, I like to cut the focaccia into bite-size squares.

PICNIC PICKLES

Serves 6-8

1 ¼ cup rice or white wine vinegar

1 cup water

1 ½ teaspoons kosher salt

2 tablespoon granulated white sugar

2 whole garlic cloves

1 tablespoon pickling spice

1 teaspoon fennel seeds

1 teaspoon fresh thyme leaves

1 teaspoon whole peppercorns

Optional:

1 red onion, thinly sliced in rings

3 cups cooked beets, diced

1 English cucumber, thinly sliced

4–5 watermelon radishes, thinly
sliced

4 rainbow carrots, cut into three-inch-
long wedges

1 pound green beans, ends trimmed

A sharp bite and tang to cut through the creaminess of cheese is sometimes what is missing on a charcuterie board. This recipe is so versatile you can pickle just about anything. It's a great activity to do when you have an abundance of produce, you will be well-stocked for a whole year of picnicking. Choose your vegetable of choice and on you go, pickling away.

Note: *This makes one jar; double if you are making two varieties. Be sure to wash and scrub the veggies well! Keep a few jars handy in the pantry for a spontaneous picnic or dinner party.*

In a small saucepan over medium heat, combine the white vinegar, water, salt, and sugar. Stir together until the sugar is dissolved.

Gather your transportation container or a 32 oz. Mason jar for each veggie. Add your prepared veggies, garlic, pickling spice, fennel seeds, thyme leaves, and whole peppercorns into the jar. You can combine a variety of the veggies together, although it's best to pickle the beets separately as they will color the rest.

Pour the mixture over the veggies until fully covered. You may need to make another batch of the brine to top it off if needed.

Let them sit for at least an hour before serving. If you have the time, let them sit overnight before your picnic. They will last about a week in the fridge.

FARMHOUSE CRACKERS

Serves 4-6

8 tablespoons cold unsalted butter,
    cut into small pieces

1 teaspoon kosher salt

1 cup white whole wheat flour

2 teaspoon white granulated sugar

¼ cup sesame seeds

¼ cup poppy seeds

¼ cup fennel seeds

¼ cup black sesame seeds

1 egg

1 tablespoon water

All-purpose flour for dusting

Maldon salt

You may wonder if it would be worth the trouble to make homemade crackers for a simple picnic, but as impressive as they sound, these are exceptionally fast to make! I'm guessing you have these ingredients already in your pantry so feel free to improvise on seeds and seasonings as you see fit.

Preparation tip: *These truly come together in no time, but they also can be made a day or two before a happy hour picnic or outing. The dough also can be stored in the fridge wrapped in plastic wrap for up to 2 to 3 days and baked up on the day of your picnic.*

Preheat the oven to 375°F. Prepare a parchment-lined baking sheet.

In a food processor or stand mixer with a paddle attachment, add the butter pieces, salt, white whole wheat flour, and sugar together. Beat on low until crumbly, about 3 minutes.

Add the seeds and mix for a minute or two on low speed until combined. Crack in the egg and mix for a few seconds until well incorporated. Scrape down the sides if necessary.

While beating on low, add a tablespoon of water and continue to mix until the dough just comes together.

Dust the parchment paper on the baking sheet with a tablespoon of flour. Take a portion of the dough and pat it down onto the paper with your hands until it forms a rough rectangle.

Roll out the dough as thin as possible on the parchment paper, about a one-eighth inch. Using a pizza slicer, cut out the crackers into any size you wish by slicing vertical and horizontal lines through the dough. Trim any excess away for an even finish on the edges. Leave the crackers on the parchment paper as they are cut; you don't need to space them apart.

Bake for 10 to 12 minutes until the edges are lightly golden. They will crisp up while they cool. Sprinkle on a pinch of Maldon salt if you wish when they come out of the oven.

Continue to cut and bake until you have used up the remaining dough. The dough can be frozen in the fridge for up to a week.

SPRING

"IT'S SPRING FEVER. THAT IS WHAT THE NAME OF IT IS. AND WHEN YOU'VE GOT IT, YOU WANT—OH, YOU DON'T QUITE KNOW WHAT IT IS YOU DO WANT, BUT IT JUST FAIRLY MAKES YOUR HEART ACHE, YOU WANT IT SO!"

—MARK TWAIN

EN PLEIN AIR

I find that the most promising and hopeful months of the year are in early spring. In Vermont, there is nothing more anxiously awaited (for most, anyway) than the arrival of spring. It is the time when stomping in the puddles and mud is completely appropriate, if not a rite of passage, as a kid. Once the horrendous trenches of mud season are long past, it is on to the greener pastures of May. With enough mud coating your boots to dress you in complete disguise, the sign of grass slowly awakening after its winter slumber is a happy day indeed. Soon to follow are the crocuses, daffodils, and of course the radiant peonies which are bright and hopeful reminders of warmer and greener days to come.

As winter loosened its cold grip, my mother would stretch her ever creative mind to find ways to give us the boot outside. When the snow melted, we'd pack a picnic by the rushing waterfalls in the backyard which flowed down heavily from the mountain. With every step on the damp grass, you can almost feel the Earth smile with delight as the sun shined just a little bit brighter and longer each day. Even now, I find that the season holds as much joy and playfulness as summer does. It is hard to describe the happy-go-lucky feeling that spring has for many New Englanders. Click your mud boots together and voilà, summer is gleefully waiting around the corner. Rain or shine, it really doesn't matter most of the time as everyone is anxious to get out for some fresh air. It's a time to dust off the old basket while in the thick of spring cleaning. After a good scrubbing, that old backpack in the closet or the dusty enamel coffee pot sitting on the top shelf will be your incentive to pack a little something when the weather calls. What is old is new come spring. Slowly but surely, a thermos of soup will transform into a cooler of watermelon spritzers on the beach.

Springtime in Hawaii is very subtle, but if you don't look at small signs, it will pass you by entirely. Rainbows pop up everywhere you look as the sleeping jacaranda trees awaken with bright violet blossoms. Regardless of where you live, let the hopeful promise of spring be a time to savor longer and brighter days. Although, perhaps forgo setting out a crisp blanket in the muddy grass unless you are as desperate for some sun as I have been known to be in mid-April. In general, springtime weather is probably the most finicky of all the four seasons so be prepared for a day when the weather simply can't make up its mind. I hope this menu will inspire the first outing of many for the deliciously warmer days to come.

RADISH & HERB BUTTER CROSTINI

Serves 6-8

1 small bunch of red or watermelon
    radishes, washed and stems
    removed
6 tablespoons high-quality salted
    butter at room temperature
2 tablespoons whole milk
2 tablespoons chives, minced
1 teaspoon tarragon, minced
1 teaspoon lemon zest
1 baguette, thinly sliced
Sunflower sprouts to garnish
Fleur de sel
Cracked black pepper
1 baguette[1]

The crisp and colorful spring radishes are one of the first things to pop up in the garden. (And one of the easiest to grow!) For a quick bite, I often slather a piece of toast with some salted butter and then layers of thinly sliced radish rounds. It is an easy and satisfying appetizer that sings spring. Pick up a baguette along the way and off you go to bask in the spring sun in a grassy meadow.

Soak the whole radishes in ice water for several hours to preserve crispness when they are sliced at the picnic site.

Meanwhile, prepare the butter spread by combining the butter, milk, herbs, and lemon zest in a stand mixer. Whip for 2 to 3 minutes until soft and creamy. Transport to a small container to pack.

Once you are ready to serve at your picnic site, thinly slice the radishes. To assemble the crostini, spread a tablespoon of the herb butter onto a slice of baguette, layer 2 to 3 radish slices on top, and garnish with sunflower sprouts. Sprinkle with pinch of fleur de sel and cracked black pepper.

»   *1 If you have the time, you can lightly toast a few of the baguette slices beforehand.*

CITRUS FENNEL SALAD

Serves 4–6

For the salad:

2 Valencia or navel oranges, reserve
      1 tablespoon of juice for dressing

1 grapefruit or pomelo

1 blood orange or 3 tangerines

2 bulbs fennel, stalks removed and
      very thinly sliced,[2] reserve a few
      fronds

4 cups baby arugula

1 sweet onion, thinly sliced

½ cup dill, roughly chopped

½ cup fresh mint, roughly chopped

For the dressing:

2 tablespoons champagne vinegar

1 tablespoon orange juice

1 teaspoon grapefruit zest

1 tablespoon wildflower honey

3 tablespoons extra virgin olive oil

½ teaspoon kosher salt

Cracked black pepper

This salad is bright, light, and oh so cheerful, similar to early days of spring. The brilliant citrus hues are a vibrant addition to any picnic spread. Sunshine on a plate when you need it! I find fennel to be a bit underappreciated but here, it's a delicious match to the zing of the citrus fruits.

Using a sharp paring knife, peel the citrus fruits and remove the white pith and skin. Cut the fruit into quarter-inch-thick rounds and set aside.

Prepare the dressing by whisking together the champagne vinegar, orange juice, grapefruit zest, and honey. Pour in the olive oil in a steady stream, whisking the dressing together until it becomes emulsified. Season with salt and cracked black pepper.

In your transportation container, add the fennel, arugula, and onions. Pour half of the dressing on top and gently toss together. Add the citrus rounds, layering them together in a pinwheel type fashion. Sprinkle on the fennel fronds, dill, and mint as you go along. Reserve few fresh sprigs to garnish for your picnic presentation.

Once you reach your picnic site, serve the salad on a shallow platter or plate and drizzle on the remaining dressing. Garnish with additional herbs.

Mixing the dressing beforehand allows the fennel to soften up and marinate. Don't worry, it won't be soggy!

»   *2 Mandoline optional*

LEMON & ASPARAGUS CAVATAPPI

Serves 6

3 tablespoons kosher salt

3 tablespoons extra virgin olive oil

1 shallot, minced

2 garlic cloves, minced

1 pound asparagus, stems trimmed
    and cut into one-inch pieces

1 cup frozen or fresh green peas

Juice of one lemon

1 teaspoon lemon zest

1 pound cavatappi or fusilli pasta

Dash of red pepper flakes

1 15 oz can cannellini beans, drained
    and rinsed

2 cups fresh baby spinach

1 cup asiago cheese, grated

Cracked black pepper

In mid-spring when the farmers markets are proudly showcasing their new greens, consider this pasta salad for your picnic rotation. I find the beauty of the spring produce is its purity, delicacy, and simplicity. The thin and tender asparagus only needs but a touch of lemon and salt to really shine. I opted to include them in addition to the peas which I find perfectly fits spring. It can be served either hot or cold which is why I love it for a springtime picnic romp.

Bring a large stock pot with 5 quarts of water with 3 tablespoons of kosher salt to a boil.

While waiting for the water to boil, add 3 tablespoons of olive oil to a large sauté pan. Add the shallots and garlic to the pan over low-medium heat. Gently sauté the shallots and garlic until they are softened about 3 minutes, stirring occasionally with a wooden spoon.

Add the asparagus and cook until the spears are tender, about 8 minutes, stirring frequently. Toss in the peas and cook for an additional 3 minutes until they are tender. Season with a pinch of salt. Stir in the lemon juice and lemon zest. Turn off the stove and set aside for now.

Once the water has come to a boil, add the pasta and cook until al dente, about 10 to 12 minutes.

Drain the pasta into a colander and transfer it right into the asparagus and peas in the sauté pan. Gently mix in the pasta with the asparagus and peas and then transfer to a large serving bowl.

In the serving bowl, add a dash of red pepper flakes, cannellini beans, and baby spinach. Drizzle a tablespoon of two of olive oil over the pasta. Combine together until the pasta is thoroughly coated.

You can either serve with freshly grated asiago cheese or mix it into the pasta once slightly cooled.

Serve with fresh cracked black pepper.

LILIKOI CHEESECAKE BITES

Makes one dozen

For the crust:

1 cup macadamia nuts

4 graham crackers

½ cup all-purpose flour

¼ cup granulated white sugar

¼ teaspoon kosher salt

6 tablespoons unsalted butter, melted

For the filling:

1½ pound cream cheese, softened at
    room temperature

½ cup sour cream, room temperature

¼ cup granulated white sugar

2 eggs, room temperature

1 egg yolk, room temperature

2 tablespoons heavy cream, room
    temperature

2 teaspoons pure vanilla extract

1 teaspoon lemon zest

For the lilikoi glaze:

4 lilikoi (passion fruit) or 1 cup passion
    fruit juice

¼ cup granulated white sugar

To garnish:

Berries

½ cup heavy cream

1 tablespoon granulated white sugar

1 teaspoon pure vanilla extract

Stewed Rhubarb:

8 oz trimmed rhubarb, cut into quarter-
    inch pieces (about 2½ cups)

½ cup granulated white sugar, plus
    more to taste if necessary

1 teaspoon orange zest

2 tablespoons water

Pinch of kosher salt

A luscious cheesecake adorned with a jewel box of berries is a classic springtime dessert in our family. When I discovered fresh lilikoi or passion fruit in Hawaii, I couldn't get enough of it with its tangy sweetness. Lip smacking lilikoi deliciously complements the creaminess of cheesecake. Rather than a full-size cake, I find these mini versions very sweet for a springtime fête and easier to transport, too. If rhubarb may be more readily available to you than lilikoi, I've included it as an equally delicious stewed substitution.

Preparation tip: *These can be made up to a day or two in advance and stored in the fridge. Pack them up when you are just about to head out the door.*

Preheat oven to 350°F and gather a small-rimmed baking sheet. Prepare a 6 or 12 cup muffin tin with paper baking cups.

Place the macadamia nuts on the baking sheet and roast for 10 minutes until slightly fragrant. Reduce the oven temperature to 325°F.

Once roasted, place the nuts and graham crackers into a food processor. Blitz for 2 to 3 minutes until the mixture resembles fine crumbs.

To prepare the crust, in a large mixing bowl, combine the macadamia nut and graham cracker mixture, flour, sugar, and salt. Slowly pour in the melted butter until thoroughly incorporated. It will be a soft and crumbly texture.

Spoon about 1 to 2 tablespoons of the crust filling into each muffin cup, pressing down with your fingers or the back of a spoon.

Begin to prepare the filling by combining the softened cream cheese and sour cream into the bowl of a stand mixer. Mix together on low for minute or two until roughly incorporated. While mixing, slowly pour in the sugar and continue for another two minutes until the mixture is no longer grainy.

Add the eggs one at a time, beating well on low after each addition. Continue to add the egg yolk, heavy cream, vanilla extract, and lemon zest. Be sure not to over beat by mixing on low speed until just incorporated.

Fill each cup to the brim of each baking paper. You may need to work in batches depending on your tin size.

Bake for 25 to 30 minutes until the sides are set but the middle is still a bit wobbly. Let them cool for 10 minutes before removing them from the molds. Once removed, allow them cool for at least another hour.

Meanwhile, prepare the lilikoi glaze by scooping out the interior of each lilikoi, pulpy seeds and all into a sieve placed over a small bowl.

Pat down and scrape the filling with a rubber spatula around the sieve to press the juice through, leaving the black seeds behind. You should have about ¾ to one cup of juice.

Add the juice and sugar to a small saucepan over medium-low heat. Slowly whisk together until the sugar has dissolved and has slightly thickened to the consistency of maple syrup.

Let the glaze cool slightly before pouring a tablespoon or so of the glaze onto the top each cheesecake. The paper cups should prevent the glaze running down the sides and hold it in place. Place the cheesecakes in the fridge, allowing the glaze to set in the fridge for 30 minutes.

Begin to prepare the garnish by pouring the heavy cream, sugar, and vanilla into bowl of a stand mixer or a small bowl if using a hand mixer. Whip on high for about 5 to 8 minutes until light and airy with soft peaks.

Once you reach your picnic site, place a small dollop of whipped cream on top of each cheesecake with a fresh berry. Be sure to keep the cheesecakes chilled in a cooler until ready to serve.

Stewed Rhubarb:

Place the rhubarb, sugar, orange zest, and water into a medium saucepan set over medium-low heat.

Bring the mixture to a simmer, stirring occasionally until the sugar has dissolved and the rhubarb becomes tender, about 10 minutes.

Using a slotted spoon, remove the rhubarb from the saucepan and transfer it into a small bowl. Continue to cook the juice until it begins to thicken and reduces down by half, about 10 minutes. Remove from the heat and transfer it into a small bowl.

Add the cooked rhubarb back into the thickened juice once it has cooled. Season with a small pinch of salt. Taste and add in more sugar if necessary, depending on your preference, I personally like it a little bit tart.

Spoon a tablespoon over each cheesecake bite when ready to serve.

ELDERFLOWER SPRITZ

Makes one cocktail

2 oz Saint Germain Elderflower Liqueur

4 oz Brut rosé sparkling wine, chilled

1 oz Sparkling soda, chilled

Berries to garnish

I couldn't think of a more delightful cocktail for spring than this floral spritzer. The elderflower is ever so subtle with the sparking rosé and leads me to imagine this would be served at the picnic in the strawberry fields of Jane Austen's *Emma*. Cheers to the blissful season of spring!

In a shaker or champagne coupe, combine the elderflower liqueur and sparkling wine.

Pour in the sparkling soda and stir well. Top with berries to garnish. Serve immediately—cheers!

SPRING SHOWERS

This book would not be complete without addressing the ever-present possibility of Plan B. Despite looking ahead in the forecast, there may be a chance that the weather will turn and what was to be a gorgeous day is now a sopping wet one. Disappointment and frustration will be felt on all accounts, to be sure. This leaves me all the more reason to stress the importance of a low key and adaptable approach to picnicking in general. Plan B may mean holding off for a day or finding a new location. However, all is not lost if you can't do either and the kids can't hide their disappointment. For those times, why not set up under a covered porch or in a small corner of the house with the blankets, pillows, and board games? It will not be the same of course, but I am sure that everyone will find it novel and amusing, nonetheless.

Even if it is pouring in gales as it often does in Maui in the spring, you can still find ways to enjoy and, dare I say, embrace it. Something cozy, comforting, and hearty sounds about right for a rainy-day menu. Whether you have a screened porch or take a drive to the local park gazebo, watching and listening to the rain is actually quite soothing, if you are staying dry of course. All is not lost. A day that would have been at the beach by no means needs to be a boring one at home with the family. With a little creativity and adaptability, a rainy day can be salvaged. Most parks have sheltered areas if you do not have a covered porch at home. If the weather isn't too horrendous, a walk to the town gazebo in a drizzle can be quite refreshing if you are properly dressed. Either way, a rainy day is what you make of it and I'll leave it at that!

KULA POT PIE

Serves 6

For biscuit topping:

3 cups all-purpose flour

1 teaspoon kosher salt

1 tablespoon baking powder

6 tablespoons unsalted butter, cold
and cut into larger pieces

1 cup whole milk plus a tablespoon or
two more, cold

1 egg yolk

1 teaspoon water

For the filling:

4 tablespoons unsalted butter

1.5 pounds Yukon gold potatoes,
about 2 cups diced

1½ cups rainbow carrots, diced into
half-inch pieces

½ cup yellow onion, diced

½ cup celery, diced

1 fresh bay leaf

1½ cup chicken stock

3 tablespoons all-purpose flour

2 cups cooked chicken, shredded into
half-inch pieces

1 cup frozen green peas

Cracked black pepper

2 teaspoon fresh thyme leaves

1 teaspoon fresh rosemary, minced

1 teaspoon fresh sage, minced

1 teaspoon kosher salt

Wet, stormy days make me crave this old-time recipe. If prepared ahead of time, you can pop them out of the freezer and reheat when it's looks like rain is on the way. Served in individual ramekins or a casserole dish, they make an otherwise dull, wet day all the more fun while warming you through and through!

__Preparation tip:__ I like to have these handy in the freezer when the occasion calls, even if it is a rainy day at home just for myself. They can be frozen for up to four to six months, believe it or not, if properly stored in the freezer. They will be ready to pull out and reheat for any sudden downpour. Reheat at 375°F for 30 to 35 minutes.

Prepare the biscuit topping by mixing together the flour, salt, and baking powder in medium mixing bowl.

Cut in the butter into the flour mixture with a pastry cutter until it resembles coarse crumbs. You can also use a food processor by pulsing the butter into the flour mixture until it forms coarse crumbs.

Pour the whole milk into the mixture, stirring it together until it forms a rough ball. Turn out the dough on a lightly floured work surface and bring the dough together with your hands, adding a tablespoon of milk if necessary until it just comes together. Be sure not to overwork it!

Keep the dough in the bowl and chill in the fridge for 30 minutes.

Meanwhile, begin to prepare the filling by add 4 tablespoons of butter to large sauté pan with a fitted lid over medium heat. Once the butter is melted, add the potatoes, carrots, onion, celery, and bay leaf. Sauté for 15 to 20 minutes, stirring frequently, until the potatoes and carrots have softened. Cover with the lid halfway through cooking, stirring occasionally.

Lower the heat and pour in the chicken stock and stir in 3 tablespoons of flour. Stir the filling until it creates a thicker, gravy-like consistency. Remove the bay leaf.

Add the shredded chicken, peas, thyme, rosemary, sage, and salt. Slowly stir the filing until everything is evenly incorporated. Season with cracked black pepper to taste.

Preheat the oven to 375°F degrees and gather 6 ovenproof ramekins. Fill each ramekin to the top with the chicken filling, about 3 tablespoons. Set aside to prep the biscuit topping.

Remove the chilled dough from the fridge and turn it out onto a lightly floured work surface. Pat down the dough with your hands into a rough rectangle about a half-inch thick.

Cut out 6 rounds, rolling out the dough again to continue cutting each biscuit out. You can also measure by placing the bottom of one ramekin on top of the dough and cutting out the impression with a knife. Place each biscuit on top of each ramekin. It should fit snuggly on each ramekin.

Prepare the egg wash by whisking the egg yolk and 1 teaspoon of water into a small bowl until foamy. Lightly brush the top of the biscuits with the egg wash.

Bake for 45 to 50 minutes until the tops are golden brown and the sides lightly bubble.

Let them cool for 15 minutes and serve warm.

Transportation Tip *Pack each pot pie wrapped in foil to keep warm. They will retain the heat on the journey when nestled together in the basket. If you decide to bring the picnic indoors, no one's the wiser!*

OATMEAL DATE BARS

Makes 8– 10 bars

For the filling:

½ cup pitted dates, about 5

½ cup dried cherries

1 cup water

¼ cup wildflower honey

½ cup golden brown sugar

½ teaspoon pure vanilla extract

Zest of one lemon

For the crust and topping:

1 ½ cups all-purpose flour

½ teaspoon kosher salt

½ cup golden brown sugar

½ cup chopped pecans

½ teaspoon ground cinnamon

10 tablespoons unsalted butter, melted

While the rain pours down, the comfort that oatmeal brings in any form is heartily appreciated. These chewy bars are homely but delicious—just what comes to mind for a sweet treat on a gloomy, wet day. While oatmeal raisin cookies may get the second pick, these won't disappoint. When stacked and wrapped together in parchment paper, what is a little rain when you are so well provisioned!

Preparation tip: *You can prep these a day or two beforehand. They also last up to 2 to 3 months in the freezer and reheat at 350°F for 20 minutes.*

Preheat the oven to 350°F. Line a nine-by-nine-inch rimmed baking tin with parchment paper, leaving a slight overhang around the rim.

Chop the dates into small half-inch pieces.

Place the chopped dates, dried cherries, water, honey, and brown sugar in a medium saucepan. Bring the filling to a boil and cook for about 5 minutes, stirring occasionally, and then lower to medium heat and continue to cook for another 10 minutes until the mixture has thickened. Once the mixture is syrupy and thickened, remove from the heat and stir in the vanilla extract and lemon zest. Set aside to cool.

Begin to prepare the crust by combining the flour, salt, brown sugar, chopped pecans, and cinnamon. Once thoroughly combined, pour in the melted butter and stir together until the mixture is evenly coated, resembling coarse crumbs. Reserve one cup of the filling and set aside.

Spread the crust into the prepared tin with parchment paper, patting down with your hands into every corner to create a smooth, even layer.

Pour in the date and cherry filling, gently spreading it evenly over the entire crust.

Sprinkle the reserved cup of crust evenly on top of the filling.

Bake for 45 minutes until golden brown. Once removed from the oven, let it cool for another 30 minutes before removing the entire square from the tin by lifting out the overhanging parchment paper. You can also let it chill in the freezer briefly if pressed for time.

Cut into bars or squares when completely cooled.

HOT BUTTERED RUM

Serves 4

2 tablespoons brown sugar

1 tablespoon wildflower honey

2 tablespoons salted butter, room
    temperature

¼ teaspoon ground cinnamon

1/8 teaspoon ground cloves

1/8 teaspoon ground nutmeg

1/8 teaspoon ground ginger

1 teaspoon orange zest

6 oz dark rum

4 cups hot apple cider

Cinnamon sticks to garnish

Optional: whipped cream

Hot buttered rum: just the sound of it makes you feel warm and cozy, especially on a wet day. It is a soothing drink that is sure to be appreciated with damp feet and cold hands. This variation includes apple cider which I find more flavorful than simply water. For a nonalcoholic alternative, simply omit the rum.

In a small bowl, combine together the brown sugar, honey, butter, spices, and orange zest until creamy.

Distribute the spiced butter mixture evenly between your serving mugs.

Pour in the dark rum equally between the mugs, about two to three tablespoons each.

Pour the hot cider into each mug and garnish with cinnamon sticks and whipped cream. Serve immediately.

Transportation Tip *Prepare the drink before you head out by storing it into a large thermos with enamel mugs or individual thermoses.*

EARLY MORNING RENDEZVOUS

The early morning hours have always been a sacred time of the day for me, which I partially owe to my father who was the only one up before dawn in our family. Rising before sunup with the steady chorus of birds outside of my window for a few quiet moments of calm sets up my day. Perhaps it's the country girl in me, but a good and fulfilling breakfast to set me up for the day is something I savor. A few slices of toast with a good pat of butter and jam or hot waffles doused with maple syrup with black tea in the morning sun is just the ticket for me. Growing up in our house, the oven and old wood stove were always working overtime in the early mornings. My mother would rise early and whip up a batch of fresh muffins or bread before she'd head out to do the barn chores. We'd take a muffin or two (or only the tops if you were my brother) and sit out in the garden together. There is simply nothing better than fresh bread or muffins slathered in good butter and enjoyed in the sunshine with hot tea.

A short drive from the cottage in Kula is one of the most spectacular spots to set out a morning spread. The sweeping view is by far one of the best of the whole island from the north to south shores. One morning, we woke up at dawn blurry eyed, packed up the car with a thermos of hot coffee and warm pastries, and headed up the winding road to catch the first rays shining over Haleakalā, lighting up the rest of the island. There is something about starting your day in the stillness of the morning with just the hum of the bees and birds that puts a smile on your face, gives a clarity of mind, and optimism in your heart.

I find that the quiet and intimacy of the morning hours is worth honoring. Sunset gets its fair share of attention for a prime time to crack open a bottle of wine with cheese, so I find sunrise is due for equal appreciation. Practically speaking, taking a quiet moment to reflect alone or with a loved one doesn't need to take a morning of planning an extravagant outing but can be created right in your backyard on a Sunday. Rolling out a blanket on the backyard lawn and toasting up some craggy English muffins while the kettle is whistling is a simple treat for a weekend morning for yourself or the family to welcome the day. Perhaps it will become a weekend ritual for you as it has for me. May this menu make it all the easier to roll out of bed!

TYNDALL HILL GRANOLA PARFAITS

Serves 4

For the granola:

4 cups old-fashioned oats

1 cup slivered almonds

¼ cup golden raisins

½ cup dried cranberries

1 cup pecans

½ cup unsweetened coconut flakes

¼ cup sesame seeds

½ cup pumpkin seeds

¼ cup all-purpose flour

1 tablespoon black strap molasses

¾ cup Vermont grade B maple syrup

1 teaspoon ground cinnamon

½ teaspoon kosher salt

1 egg white, beaten until frothy

For yogurt parfaits:

6 cups vanilla Greek yogurt

2 cups Tyndall Hill granola

3 cups fresh berries such as
    strawberries, blueberries,
    raspberries, and blackberries

2–3 tablespoons wildflower honey

Named after the hill above our farm, this granola is really the star of the show here. I grew up on this hearty granola as we were never allowed boxed ones—or anything processed, for that matter. It consists of pantry staples and keeps for a long while. A wholesome mix of nuts, seeds, and dried fruit make an excellent topping for tangy Greek yogurt and berries. I'm partial to the crispy clumps which I may have dig out, but who's watching anyway.

Preheat the oven to 350°F. Prepare a fifteen-by-ten-inch rimmed baking sheet with parchment paper.

In a large mixing bowl, combine together the oats, almonds, raisins, dried cranberries, pecans, coconut flakes, sesame seeds, and pumpkin seeds. Mix thoroughly until evenly dispersed.

Add in the flour, molasses, maple syrup, cinnamon, salt, and the beaten egg white. Stir until thoroughly combined.

Pour out the granola on to the parchment paper, spreading it evenly with a wooden spoon.

Bake for about 15 minutes, then pull it out of the oven turning it only to brown the other side and then bake for an additional 15 minutes until golden brown and crisp. You can break the larger pieces down into smaller bits if you wish.

For yogurt parfaits:

In a weck or Mason jar with a screw top lid, fill half of the jar with yogurt. Top with a tablespoon or two with granola, fresh berries, and a drizzle of honey. For an extra special touch, garnish with colorful edible flowers.

OLD-FASHIONED ENGLISH MUFFINS

Makes 8-10 English Muffins

4½ cups bread flour

1 tablespoon golden brown sugar

1½ cup whole milk

2¼ teaspoons active dry yeast

1 egg

½ teaspoon kosher salt

3 tablespoons unsalted butter, softened

1 cup cornmeal

We'd pick them right up, piping hot, off the griddle. These cannot compare to anything store bought with their soft and craggy crumb soaking up pools of butter and jam. They are a wonderful alternative to morning toast for a breakfast on the go. Pass the butter, please!

Preparation tip: *Rather than rising early in the wee hours of the morning to bake up a fresh batch, you can bake them a day or two beforehand and toast them before you head out.*

Using a stand mixer with paddle attachment, combine the bread flour, sugar, whole milk, yeast, egg, salt, and butter into the mixing bowl. This dough will be a bit stickier, and I find the paddle attachment works best.

Knead the bread for about 8 minutes on low-medium speed until it forms a rough sticky ball that is elastic and shiny. It should slightly pull away from the sides of the bowl.

Place the dough out onto a clean work surface and shape it into a rough ball and place it in a clean bowl, lightly oiled with a neutral cooking spray. Let the dough rise for 1½ to 2 hours in a warm place. Line a baking sheet with parchment paper. Sprinkle cornmeal on the baking sheet.

Once the dough has risen, take out the dough and put it out on a lightly floured work surface. Using a dough scraper, cut out 10 equal sized pieces.

Shape each piece into a ball by cupping the dough and pulling in toward you, sliding it along the table to form a taught surface. You may have to repeat a few times until it makes a tidy ball.

Place the ball on the baking sheet and pat it down to form a circle about three inches in diameter, about a quarter- to a half-inch thick, coating one side with cornmeal.

Flip it over and pat down again to coat the second side with cornmeal. Continue to roll out the rest of the dough. Let them rise for another 30 minutes. They should be soft and puffy.

Preheat the oven to 350°F. Heat a large cast-iron pan or griddle to low-medium heat. Once warmed, place as many English muffins as can fit on the griddle without any touching each other, leaving about one inch between each. Grill the English muffins for 6 to 8 minutes on each side, using a spatula to flip once golden brown.

Place the grilled English muffins on the baking sheet. Continue grilling the rest, placing them all on the baking sheet. Bake for another 10 to 15 minutes to continue to cook the interior. They should sound hollow if you gently tap them.

To serve, gently tear the English muffins open using a fork or your fingers to pry them apart. They also keep for several days and freeze well, too, if you decide to make a batch beforehand.

GRUYÈRE & SPINACH TART

1 ½ cup all-purpose flour

1 teaspoon kosher salt

½ teaspoon granulated white sugar

8 tablespoons cold unsalted butter, cut into small pieces

¼ cup ice water plus a tablespoon or more if needed

3 strips smoked bacon, roughly chopped

2 tablespoons extra virgin olive oil

½ cup red onions, diced

2 cups spinach, chopped

4 eggs

1 tablespoon crème fraîche

Cracked blacked pepper

¼ cup Gruyère cheese, shredded

A quiche may be an old tried and true dish, but it really couldn't be more ideal for an early morning breakfast. It can be served either hot or cold, or filled and baked in the early morning before heading out the door. The recipe also is very forgiving as you can use whatever you have in the fridge, be it spinach, collards, ham, or cheddar. The pastry dough can also be stored for up to a week in the freezer and rolled out when needed. As impressive as it looks, it is quite simple.

Preparation tip: *You can prepare the tart tin with the frozen pastry dough only, wrapping it properly to keep in the freezer to pull out the night before.*

In a medium sized bowl, add combine the flour, ½ teaspoon of the salt, and sugar. Using a pastry cutter, cut the butter pieces into the flour mixture until it resembles coarse crumbs. You can also use a food processor and pulse everything together, adding the water gradually until the butter is in pea-size bits.

Slowly add the ice water to the bowl, bringing it roughly together with your hands. Turn out the dough onto a work surface adding a tablespoon or two more ice water, just enough bring it together in a rough ball. Try not to over work it by cupping it in your hands, gently bringing the remaining flour and butter bits together.

Wrap the dough in plastic wrap and chill for 30 minutes in the freezer or overnight in the fridge.

Meanwhile, warm a large sauté pan over medium-low heat. Add the bacon pieces and cook for about 8 to 10 minutes over medium heat until crisp. Using a spoon, place the bacon on a paper towel-lined plate and use another sheet to soak up the extra fat. Set aside.

In another large sauté pan, add the olive oil and red onions. Sauté for about 15 minutes, stirring occasionally, until the onions are softened.

Add the spinach and cook for another 5 minutes until wilted, stirring to incorporate the onions and bacon. Set aside to cool.

Preheat the oven to 350°F. Gather a nine-inch diameter fluted tart tin and lightly grease it with a nonstick spray.

if you need. Place the dough into the tin, forming it alongside the grooves with your fingers leaving a little excess pastry hanging over the edge. You can use a small ball of excess pastry to help you tuck in the pastry into the grooves. Next, using a rolling pin, gently roll over the edge of the tin to cut away the excess, leaving a clean rim.

Prick the inside of the tart bottom with a fork a few times.

Line the tin with foil, getting it lined in every crack as best as you can and fill with baking beans or dried beans.

Chill the tart crust for an additional half hour in the freezer.

Once chilled, remove it from the freezer and blind bake the crust for 15 minutes.

After the initial 15 minutes, remove the baking beans and parchment paper. Continue to bake for another 10 to 12 minutes until the pastry is golden and a bit drier. Remove from the oven and set aside to prepare the filling.

In a small bowl, whisk together 4 eggs and the crème fraîche until frothy and light. Season with ½ teaspoon of salt and cracked black pepper. Transfer the egg mixture into a small pitcher or liquid measuring cup so it will be easier to pour.

To fill the tart, scoop a tablespoon or two of the spinach and bacon filling on the bottom, spread evenly. Next, slowly pour the egg mixture to fill the tart just below the brim. Generously sprinkle Gruyère cheese on top with fresh cracked pepper.

Bake for 25 to 30 minutes until golden and the filling is set. Let the tart cool for a few minutes before removing it from the tin.

GREEN MOUNTAIN CRUMB CAKE

Rising up bright and early to catch the sunrise may take a little more effort for some but this coffee cake will get you leaping out of bed. Perhaps it's the Vermonter in me, but I love the flavor of maple in the morning. It's warm and comforting, especially spiced up with cinnamon and toasty nuts. You'll be picking away at this cake the rest of the day, I promise you.

Preparation tip: *Bake this cake a day in advance if you need to and hardly anyone will be able to tell the difference. Gently warm it at 350°F with a foil wrapping for 15 minutes or so before packing up.*

For the cake:

2 cups all-purpose flour

1 teaspoon ground cinnamon

¼ teaspoon ground nutmeg

1 teaspoon kosher salt

1 teaspoon baking powder

1 teaspoon baking soda

8 tablespoons unsalted butter at room temperature

¾ cup dark brown sugar

½ cup maple syrup, preferably Vermont Grade B

2 eggs

1 teaspoon pure vanilla extract

1 cup sour cream

¼ cup whole milk

For the filling and topping:

1 cup all-purpose flour

½ cup brown sugar

¼ cup maple sugar

¼ teaspoon kosher salt

1 tablespoon ground cinnamon

¼ cup chopped walnuts

¼ cup chopped pecans

¼ cup old-fashioned oats

6 tablespoons unsalted butter, melted

Preheat the oven to 350°F. Grease a nine-by-nine-inch square or circle cake tin or baking dish.

In a medium sized mixing bowl, combine together the flour, cinnamon, nutmeg, kosher salt, baking powder, and baking soda.

Using a stand mixer with paddle attachment, cream together the butter, dark brown sugar, and maple syrup.

Add one egg at a time, beating well after each addition. Add the vanilla, sour cream, and milk, and mix on medium speed for one minute until well-combined.

Working in batches, gradually add the flour mixture, beating well after each addition and scraping down the sides. Set aside to make the filling and topping.

To create the filling: in a small bowl, combine together the flour, brown sugar, maple sugar, salt, cinnamon, walnuts, and pecans. The oats and butter will be mixed into the topping later.

Pour half of the batter into the prepared pan and sprinkle a quarter of the filling to cover the batter evenly.

Pour the remaining batter over the filling.

To make the topping, add the oats and melted butter to the remaining filling, combining well until it is all evenly coated with butter. Sprinkle the topping over the cake evenly.

Bake for 50 to 60 minutes or until a knife comes out clean when inserted in the center.

AN INVITATION TO TEA

I can't think of a more appropriate time for an afternoon tea picnic than in the spring. The new budding blooms and the fresh green grass awakening in the warm sun are the perfect backdrop for a hot cup.

When I was younger, my sister Olivia and I would pluck pillows from the couch, the best linen tablecloth we could find, and the good china from the cabinet (all without my mother's knowing, of course) and set up a little tea picnic under the birch trees. We created a mixed-and-matched bouquet from the garden and set it up on a pile of old books that became our makeshift table. We attempted to be as fancy and proper as possible, whatever that may have been in our young minds. We were just two little girls sitting under the shade of a birch tree, having afternoon tea of oatmeal cookies with grass-stained feet, without a care in the world.

Now years later, I've made it a priority to set time aside for myself in the later afternoon. Pausing over a hot black tea with a little something sweet in the late afternoon has been a habit I've come to look forward to everyday. A moment of self-care replenishes my focus.

For me, the notion of afternoon tea isn't something as proper or traditional as is often pictured, but rather an opportunity of self-care to reconnect to yourself or a good friend. It's fun to play up the historical traditions of the ritual, but I find that the most valuable takeaway is creating a time and space to reset and cherish company of good friends or oneself. A comforting cup of tea can be so simple yet set things right at the same time. Although setting a table outside for tea may not seem like something for the average day, it is fun to take out the china and put it to use on a whim, especially on a sunny spring day with a table and a few chairs or a picnic table. You can make it as elaborate or simple as you like. A few flowers, a tea set (borrowed, or your own, dusted off), and some sweet and savory goodies is all it really is. Oh, and hot tea, of course.

I hope this menu inspires you to call up an old friend, invite them over for a treat, and talk about anything and everything—even down to the very trivial. What matters is the care and consideration of your attention and open ear.

WINSLOW'S TEA SANDWICHES

Serves 6-8

Cucumber & Radish

High-quality salted butter, softened

1 tablespoon chives, minced

Cracked black pepper

8 slices soft wheat bread

1 English cucumber, thinly sliced

6–8 red radishes, thinly sliced

Salmon & Dill

½ cup cream cheese softened

3 tablespoons fresh dill, minced

1 tablespoon chives, minced

½ teaspoon kosher salt

Juice of ½ a lemon or 1 tablespoon
   lemon juice

8 slices rye bread

Cracked black pepper

½ pound smoked salmon, sliced

Chicken & Pecan Salad

½ cup cream cheese

3 tablespoons unsalted butter,
   softened

¼ cup pecans, lightly toasted and
   finely chopped

3 strips smoked bacon, cooked and
   crumbled

1 large chicken breast or 2 cups of
   chicken, finely chopped

2 tablespoon tarragon, finely
   chopped

3 tablespoons chives, minced

¼ cup dried cranberries, finely
   chopped

4 tablespoons extra virgin olive oil-
   based mayonnaise

½ teaspoon kosher salt

Cracked black pepper to taste

8 slices seeded or nut wheat bread

Sandwiches paired with robust and seeded breads adds flavorful dimension as opposed to the traditional soft white which can be quite bland. I named them after my mischievous pup Winslow, who has yet to pass his manners class and snuck one off the plate in glee.

Cucumber & Radish

Combine the butter and chives together in a bowl. Using a wooden spoon, beat the butter with the chives lightly to create a creamy and soft consistency. Crack some fresh black pepper over it and set aside.

To assemble the sandwich, smear a tablespoon of butter on 4 slices of the bread. Alternate layering the cucumber and radishes on top of the butter. Spread another layer of butter on the remaining 4 slices. Top of the sandwich with the second slice, butter side down. Remove the crusts with a bread knife. Cut the sandwiches into quarters or rectangles.

Salmon & Dill

Combine the cream cheese, fresh dill, chives, salt, and lemon juice together in a bowl. Using a wooden spoon, whip the mixture lightly to create a creamy consistency. Crack some fresh black pepper over it and set aside.

To assemble the sandwich, smear a tablespoon of the cream cheese on 4 slices of bread. Layer slices of salmon on the cream cheese. On the remaining 4 slices, spread a layer of cream cheese evenly. Top the remaining slices on to create a sandwich, cream cheese side down on the salmon. Remove the crusts with a bread knife. Cut the sandwiches into quarters or rectangles.

Chicken & Pecan Salad

> ***Preparation tip:*** *As the other two combinations are fairly simple, for time saving purposes, you can prepare the filling a day in advance and assemble the day of.*

In a small mixing bowl, combine the cream cheese and butter until it smooth and creamy. Set aside for now. In another medium mixing bowl, add the pecans, bacon, chicken, tarragon, chives, cranberries, and mayonnaise. Season with salt and cracked black pepper to taste.

Spread a dollop or two on four slices of bread. Top with the second slice and gently press down. Remove the crusts with a bread knife. Cut the sandwiches into quarters or rectangles.

CHERRY CREAM SCONES

Makes 14–16 scones

½ cup chopped dried cherries

¼ cup fresh orange juice

¼ teaspoon pure almond extract

3 cups all-purpose flour

1 tablespoon baking powder

½ teaspoon kosher salt

1 cup raw cane sugar

1 ½ cup heavy cream plus two
    tablespoons

Turbinado sugar

For how homely these ingredients are, they make quite delectable and elegant scones. Using a scallop cutter elevates an otherwise basic biscuit shape. Generously slather on your choice of butter, jam, or cream, and then you off you trot with a spread fit for a queen.

Preparation tip: *You can prep these a day in advance if needed or they can be kept in the freezer for up to two months and reheated when you have an unexpected afternoon guest.*

Preheat the oven to 375°F. Prepare a parchment-lined baking sheet.

In a small bowl, add the dried cherries, orange juice, and almond extract. Let the mixture sit for 15 minutes.

Meanwhile, in a separate bowl, combine the flour, baking powder, salt, and sugar. Mix together until thoroughly combined.

Add the soaked cherries to the flour mixture. Gradually pour in the heavy cream, stirring with each addition. It should resemble a rough shaggy ball. Add more cream, if necessary, to form a cohesive dough. It should not be sticky, but wet enough to just bring the dry ingredients together.

On a lightly floured work surface, place the dough and pat it down until it forms a rough circle about three-quarter-inches thick.

Using a scalloped pastry cutter that is at least two inches in diameter, cut out the scones and reform the dough into a circle as you go to continue cutting out scones. Place the scones on the baking sheet.

If you have the time, place the scones in the freezer for a half hour, which ensures a good crumb. Otherwise, you can bake them as is.

Using a pastry brush or a spoon with your finger, gently brush the top with little bit of heavy cream. Lightly sprinkle the top with turbinado sugar.

Bake for 15 to 20 minutes until light golden brown. Serve warm with fresh jam, clotted cream, or butter.

JEWEL DROPS

2 cups all-purpose flour

1 cup almond flour

1 teaspoon baking powder

½ teaspoon kosher salt

16 tablespoons (2 sticks) unsalted
     butter at room temperature

½ cup granulated white sugar

1 ½ teaspoons pure almond extract

1 teaspoon orange zest

Powdered sugar for dusting

Jam preserves such as raspberry,
     strawberry, blueberry, or orange
     marmalade

What little gems these cookies are. Filled with colorful jam and preserves, they couldn't be simpler to make yet look like jewels on a plate. The orange zest paired with the almond flavor complements the buttery texture that's as tempting as precious stones themselves. Also, any baker knows dusting a little powdered sugar always makes for a pretty finish if all else fails!

Preparation tip: *These can be made up to 2 to 3 days in advance of your afternoon tea.*

Preheat the oven to 350°F and line a baking sheet with parchment paper.

In a small mixing bowl, combine the flour, almond flour, baking powder, and salt.

Using a stand mixture with a paddle attachment, cream the butter and sugar together until it's pale and creamy.

Add the almond extract and orange zest, mixing only until thoroughly combined.

Slowly and gradually add the flour mixture on low speed to the stand mixing bowl of butter and sugar, scraping down the sides until it comes into a cohesive dough.

Using your hands or a spoon, roll out a half-inch ball of dough and place on the baking sheet.

After rolling out all of the dough, using your index finder, gently make a quarter-inch indentation onto the top of each ball. Continue with the rest of the dough. Refrigerate the cookies for 15 minutes to harden up the shape.

Bake for about 10 minutes and remove the cookies to reshape the indentation. Use a small teaspoon to gently repress down the original fingerprint. Continue to bake for another 8 minutes until lightly golden.

Remove the cookies from the sheet to a wire rack to cool completely. Once cooled, lightly dust with powdered sugar. These will be quite delicate to handle.

Fill the indent with a small ½ teaspoon of jam preserves. Vary the types of jams you use to fill the cookies for a brightly colored selection.

SUMMER BERRY CAKES

1¾ cups all-purpose flour

1 teaspoon baking powder

½ teaspoon kosher salt

8 tablespoons unsalted butter, softened

¾ cup granulated white sugar

4 eggs, room temperature

1 tablespoon pure vanilla extract

3 teaspoons whole milk

1 cup heavy cream

2 tablespoons powdered sugar

1 vanilla pod, scraped

¾ cup raspberry jam

¾ cup thinly sliced strawberries

Powdered sugar for dusting

¼ cup berries to garnish (optional)

These sweet little cakes are an absolute treat for an afternoon pick-me-up or tea with a friend. It is a classic tea cake that will not disappoint, especially with the ripe and juicy summer berries with dollops of cream. Don't mind if I do!

Preparation tip: *You can bake the cakes a day beforehand and assemble on the day of your tea party.*

Preheat the oven to 350°F. Lightly grease a 6 or 12 cup mini cake tin.

In a medium sized mixing bowl, combine the flour, baking powder, and salt. Using a stand mixer with paddle attachment, beat the butter and sugar together on medium speed until creamy. Crack the eggs into the batter one at a time, beating about 30 seconds after each addition. Scrape down the sides of the mixing bowl with a rubber spatula as needed. Add in the vanilla extract and milk, beating a minute or so until incorporated.

Slowly add the flour mixture, gradually adding a little bit at a time. Scrape down the sides of the bowl and beat on medium speed for about a minute or two until well incorporated.

Divide the batter between the cups in the tin evenly. Level the top with a rubber spatula. Bake for 15 minutes until golden or until an inserted toothpick comes out clean. Let the cakes cool for a minute or two in the tins, then remove and transfer them to a wire rack to cool completely.

Meanwhile, prepare the whipped cream by adding the cup of heavy cream, powdered sugar, and scraped vanilla beans to a clean mixing bowl with a whisk attachment. Whisk the heavy cream for about 8 to 10 minutes until it forms billowy but firm peaks.

Once the cakes are cool, using a serrated knife, cut each cake in half evenly through the center.

Spread a tablespoon of jam on the bottom half. Follow with a dollop of whipped cream. Layer on a few slices of thin strawberries. Top the cake with the second half and lightly dust powdered sugar over the top of the cake. For additional decoration, continue to place a teaspoon of whipped cream on top and place a blueberry or another berry of your choice on the cream.

Assemble the cakes just before serving to keep the whipped cream fresh. Serve the cakes immediately or lightly chilled. You can prepare the cakes the day before or freeze them if you wish and then assemble them when you are ready to serve tea.

SUMMER

"REST IS NOT IDLENESS, AND TO LIE SOMETIMES ON THE GRASS UNDER TREES ON A SUMMER'S DAY, LISTENING TO THE MURMUR OF THE WATER, OR WATCHING THE CLOUDS FLOAT ACROSS THE SKY, IS BY NO MEANS A WASTE OF TIME."

—JOHN LUBBOCK,
THE USE OF LIFE

UPCOUNTRY LUNCH

There is nothing quite like summer on the farm in the mountains. When I return home, I dig right in and marvel at all the beautiful vegetables that hide in the greenery. The tomato vines drip with crimson and golden globes and some of the bigger heirloom plants can barely support their irregularly shaped fruit. I pick whatever looks ripe and ready to be harvested and pile the garden loot on an antique table in the barn. One afternoon, I wandered down the rows picking some greens and tomatoes for lunch. As I gathered my finds on the table, I thought, why not prepare it right here? I saw the makings of a wonderful panzanella salad with olive oil, tons of homegrown garlic, tomatoes, and freshly picked herbs.

When it was time to eat, we sat down in the old Adirondack chairs facing the pond and took a moment to enjoy the peace. We sipped, talked, and admired all the beauty around with a glass of wine in hand. There is nothing quite as rewarding as a picnic straight from the abundant bounty of the summer garden.

Now that I am newly settled into a little country cottage at the foothills of the majestic Haleakalā Crater, I feel like I have created my own haven that reminds me of home. Complete with a fruit orchard, olive trees, and old horse stable, my quirky little cottage is the peace and space I have yearned for since moving to Hawaii. The enormous yet neglected garden was overrun with thick grass and brambles. After stumbling upon an old wooden wheelbarrow in the barn with "Old Country Carts Made in Vermont" carved into the side, I knew this place was meant to be. I took it upon myself as a project to clear and prepare the forgotten beds for planting. Ripping out thickly rooted blackberries and ginger was extremely laborious and exhausting work. With blood, sweat, and some tears, it is now brimming with new roses, tomatoes, herbs, and all sorts of beautiful vegetables.

This menu and story are a celebration of home and the summer garden. It celebrates the soul-gratifying reward of planting and growing your own food at home. After months of hard work, sharing a picnic harvested straight from your own garden in the dappled sunlight is one of life's simple joys.

HERB POTATO SALAD WITH LEMON VINAIGRETTE

Serves 6

For the salad:

2 pounds red potatoes or a variety of blue and Yukon gold, washed and scrubbed

2 cups sugar snap peas

1 medium red onion, thinly sliced

2 tablespoons fresh thyme leaves

1 cup fresh Italian parsley, chopped

¾ cup fresh chives, minced

Lemon wedges and thyme sprigs to garnish

For the vinaigrette:

2 tablespoons fresh lemon juice

3 tablespoons champagne vinegar

1 tablespoon whole grain mustard

1 garlic clove, minced

½ teaspoon thyme leaves

1 teaspoon lemon zest

½ teaspoon kosher salt

½ cup extra virgin olive oil

Cracked black pepper to taste

Rustling up fresh herbs from the garden for a dish is always a treat. I love gathering handfuls of the aromatic herbs to uplift summery dishes such as these creamy potatoes and crunchy snap peas. With a zing of lemon, it tastes as bright and green as the season itself. The summer farmer's markets are brimming with bundles of fresh herbs. You can also substitute whatever herbs you have on hand.

Preparation tip: This salad tastes even better when prepped in advance. You can make the entire salad a day ahead of time; the flavors really set in as the potatoes absorb the dressing and herbs.

Leave the potato skins on and cut them into halves. Bring a 5-quart pot with water to a boil for potatoes. Cook potatoes for about 2 minutes and reduce to medium heat for 12 to 15 minutes until they are tender when pierced with a knife. Drain in a colander and leave them to chill in the fridge.

In a small pot with 3 cups of water, boil the sugar snap peas shelled for about 3 minutes to blanch them. Drain immediately and rinse with cold water to stop them from cooking. They should be tender but snappy. Set aside for now.

To make the vinaigrette, whisk together the lemon juice, champagne vinegar, mustard, garlic, thyme, lemon zest, and salt in a small mixing bowl. While whisking, slowly pour in the olive oil until the dressing is emulsified. Season with cracked black pepper to taste. Pack away in a sealed jar and shake well upon serving.

Transfer the potatoes, red onions, sugar snap peas, fresh thyme, parsley, and chives to your transportation container. Reserve a few peas to garnish. Gently toss with vinaigrette once at the picnic site. Garnish with peas, a drizzle of olive oil, chives, fresh sprigs of thyme, and lemon wedges.

Note: For an extra touch, chive blossoms are edible! Leaving a few peas shelled with some pea shoots on top adds a touch of garden whimsy.

SWEET & SAVORY TARTINES

Serves 6–8

Sweet Toppings:

Ricotta

Cream cheese

Goat cheese

Burrata

Figs

Fresh berries

Red grapes

Peaches

Plums

Passion fruit

Pears

Pomegranate seeds

Honey

Jam

Mint

Savory Toppings:

Pesto

Basil

Thyme

Sautéed broccoli rabe

Roasted peppers

Heirloom tomatoes

Roasted cherry tomatoes

Olive tapenade

Roasted garlic

Radishes

Cucumbers

Smoked salmon

Cured meats

Brie

Blue cheese (Roquefort, Stilton)

Sharp cheddar

Pickled red onion

Anyone who knows me well enough is aware of my unabashed love for good bread. Toasted or straight out of the oven—yes, please! A hearty and rustic loaf is the perfect blank canvas to pile on scrumptious and creative toppings. Tartines are a fun way to offer variety and everyone can contribute their favorite toppings. You can tuck right in with your hands—knife and fork optional!

Preparation tip: Gather and prepare your toppings a day in advance so that you have one less detail to think about on the day of your picnic. Organize the toppings in your cooler and basket by keeping all similar ingredients together. If you have your favorite topping combinations in mind already, you can pack them together in your cooler for an easier assembly. Use the original containers or Mason jars to pack pesto, spreads, honey, roasted peppers, jams, and tapenades. Once at the picnic site, you can transfer them to small bowls if you wish. Keep berries and cheeses in their original packaging until picnic time. Slice the fruit at the picnic site to keep it fresh. The toasts are best grilled the day of your picnic so that they are fresh, crispy, and still warm.

Prepare the bread slices just before you head out. Turn on the broiler. Slice bread into half-inch slices and arrange and them in a single layer on a rimmed baking sheet. Using a pastry brush or spoon, lightly brush slices with extra virgin olive oil.

Toast them for 3 to 5 minutes, turning once, until they are golden brown. Keep them warm and wrapped in aluminum foil until serving at the picnic location.

Assemble toppings of your choosing. Have an assortment of cheese and butter knives for spreading. Bring anything else you love or whatever is in your fridge to mix together creatively. Nearly anything is good on toasted bread. The messier, the better!

Suggested Sweet Topping Combinations: Ricotta, red grapes, figs, honey, and thyme, Burrata, peaches, honey, and mint, Goat cheese, passion fruit, honey, and mint, Blue cheese, figs, and honey

Suggested Savory Topping Combinations: Burrata, heirloom tomatoes, and basil with balsamic vinegar, Pesto, roasted cherry tomatoes, and parmesan cheese shavings, Ricotta, prosciutto, peach, honey, and thyme, Cream cheese, smoked salmon, cucumber, radish, and dill, Ricotta, sautéed broccoli rabe, and roasted garlic

GARDEN PANZANELLA SALAD

Serves 4-6

Day-old country or artisan loaf,
    roughly torn into one- to two-inch
    pieces
½ cup pine nuts
3–4 ripe tomatoes (such as Cherokee
    purple, roma, brandywine, and
    sungold), diced
1 red onion, thinly sliced
2–3 garlic cloves, minced
1–2 cups basil, roughly chopped
¼ cup fresh oregano, roughly
    chopped
½ cup extra virgin olive oil, plus more
    if necessary
¼ cup balsamic vinegar
½ teaspoon kosher salt
Cracked black pepper

One of my favorite things is a good, crusty bread. Paired with tomatoes and herbs harvested from the garden, the crisp bread soaks up the sweet juices and oil, leaving you sopping up every drop. It is a wonderful salad to improvise with using other fresh vegetables or herbs in your garden and is best prepared on the day of your picnic. Although this salad is simple, try and source the best quality ingredients you can find, including the bread!

Preheat the oven to 350°F.

Toss the bread pieces in a large bowl with a tablespoon or two of olive oil lightly coating them. Spread them onto a baking tray and toast them for 10 to 15 minutes, turning them once to toast evenly until golden and crispy.

In a cast-iron pan over low-medium heat, add the pine nuts and toast them just for 3 to 5 minutes until fragrant as they burn easily.

In a large bowl, toss in the tomatoes, toasted bread pieces, red onion, garlic, herbs, and pine nuts.

Drizzle with the olive oil and balsamic vinegar. Season with salt and pepper to taste and serve immediately.

OLIVE OIL CAKE WITH SUMMER PEACHES & THYME

Serves 6

2 ripe peaches, thinly sliced

¼ cup wildflower honey, reserve one tablespoon

1 cup extra virgin olive oil, reserve one tablespoon

¾ cup brown sugar

3 eggs

2 cups all-purpose flour

1 teaspoon baking soda

1 teaspoon baking powder

½ teaspoon kosher salt

1 teaspoon pure almond extract

1 tablespoon water (if necessary)

Powdered sugar

3–4 thyme sprigs

Wildflower honey to garnish

In high summer in Vermont, there is a small Mennonite family farm down the road from our home that ships up juicy, swollen peaches from their Amish relatives in rural Pennsylvania. At least once a week, I would hop on my bike and fill up my backpack with as many as I could carry for the several mile ride. This cake is an ode to those sweet summer memories.

Preparation tip: The cake itself can be baked a day in advance; it will still be moist and fresh. Use a tea towel to keep it covered overnight on a cooling rack or cutting board. The whipped cream can be made a day before, too, just be sure to keep it in the fridge and give it a fresh whip the day of your picnic. Use a sturdy cake carrier with a handle and bring along the edible flowers and thyme to decorate if it's easier for you. Don't forget a jar of honey for a last-minute drizzle.

Preheat the oven at 350°F and grease a nine-inch round cake pan with olive oil.

In a small bowl, toss together the peach slices with the reserved tablespoon of honey and reserved tablespoon of olive oil and set aside.

In another bowl, whisk the eggs, remaining cup of olive oil, brown sugar, and honey until thoroughly combined and slightly foamy.

Combine the dry ingredients of flour, baking soda, baking powder, and salt together in a separate bowl.

Slowly add the flour mixture to the whisked egg mixture until thoroughly combined. Continue to add in the almond extract and tablespoon of water if the batter is a little thick. (The thickness depends on the viscosity of your honey.)

Gently fold the peaches into the batter, reserving 5 to 6 slices to place in the base of the cake pan.

Create a circular fan-like pattern with the remaining peach slices on the base of the cake pan. Gently pour the batter on top into the pan and bake for 35 to 40 minutes until rich golden brown and an inserted knife comes out clean.

Once the cake is completely cooled, sprinkle with powdered sugar and thyme sprigs. Decorate with fresh nasturtiums or other edible flowers you like. Serve with fresh homemade whip cream or vanilla bean ice cream.

AUGUST LEMONADE

Serves 6

3 large peaches, pitted and cut into
     ½ inch slices

6 cups water, reserve 1 cup

1 ½ cup granulated white sugar

1 cup fresh lemon juice

½ cup fresh mint

Lemon and peach slices to garnish

In the late summer months in Maui, there are a few wild peach trees in the backyard that drip to the ground with juicy ripe fruit. Albeit smaller than their larger cousins, they are the perfect balance of sweetness and tartness. Paired with bright lemons, they make a refreshing sip under the summer sun. This recipe works wonderfully with any stone fruit you prefer.

Preparation tip: Any lemonade is best served freshly squeezed as the liquids and sugars haven't begun to separate. This will taste the brightest and sweetest when juiced fresh with the peaches. Combine the peach mixture and water before you reach the picnic site in a glass or plastic jug. You can keep the peach, lemon slices, and mint in a separate container. Once you reach your picnic site, transfer lemonade to a glass or clear pitcher and add the garnishes.

In a small saucepan, bring one cup of water, sugar, and the peach slices to a boil. Reduce to medium low heat for 5 minutes until peaches are tender and soft. Let the mixture cool and set aside.

Place the stewed peaches in a blender and blitz until smooth, about a minute. You can pour this mixture through a sieve if you like (I prefer the peachy bits).

In a serving pitcher, pour in the peach juice, lemon juice, and remaining cups of water. You can use sparkling water if you wish too! Taste and adjust the sweetness or tartness with sugar to your preference.

Refrigerate until chilled to your desire. Fill glasses with ice and garnish with mint leaves and peach or lemon slices.

LA DOLCE VITA

One summer, I spent a month exploring Italy, from the cobbled and ancient streets of Rome to the rugged Almalfi coastline of the south. The cool early mornings and late afternoons were the ideal time to wander into the little shops that sold every type of pasta shape imaginable.

I escaped the heat, dodging the zippy scooters of Rome, and headed south. The rugged hillside was dotted with stoic cypress and olive trees—witnesses to generations of Italian history. The drive that unfolded before me with winding bends and climbs along the coast was absolutely breathtaking. The salty breeze and deep lapis blue ocean were a refreshing sight and smell in contrast to the sweltering streets of Rome. The seafood, *frutti di mare,* was exceptionally fresh and caught merely a few hours before it was swimming on my plate in Tuscan olive oil with fresh Sicilian lemon. Overall, I was simply amazed at how simple and homely ingredients could be transformed into something so luscious and indulgent. The sweet and bulbous tomatoes dressed with sea salt and peppery olive oil were sublime. I felt a connection to the way the Italians cook and revere food.

That's when my wonder and appreciation for the flavors of the Mediterranean began. I find that there is something idyllic and romantic about it that conjures up feelings of absolute idleness, pleasure, and a feast for the senses. The simplest of pleasures were by no means guilty ones. They were necessities, in fact, which I of course happily adopted.

When I was staying with my Italian friend's family, I discovered the jovial-yet-dramatic Italian table. I found that whether someone was in the kitchen stirring something delicious in a large pot, taking sips of red wine mid-sentence, or at large outdoor family picnic, connection and conversation is at the heart of the culture, a moveable feast if there ever was one. Whether it's possible to hear each other while people talk over one another is another story, but being together as a family is what mattered most. Regardless of how heated it got, sitting down together for meals outside was a ritual. The quiet introvert that I am, I equally savored the solo moments of peace under the shade of an olive tree, listening to the soft hum of bees with an ice-cold gelato. My time in Italy taught me that it's the simple things that truly count.

CITRUS MARINATED OLIVES

Serves 6–8

3–4 cups mixed olives such as Kalamata or Castelvetrano

2 garlic cloves, minced

¼ cup fresh rosemary, minced

¼ cup fresh thyme leaves

¼ cup fresh oregano, minced

Juice of one orange (peel a few strips before)

Juice of one grapefruit (peel a few strips before)

Red pepper flakes

Extra virgin olive oil

Cracked black pepper

It wouldn't be a Mediterranean picnic without the iconic olive. I've always had a salty palate over a sweet one and these are a beautiful blend of both. The fresh, sweet citrus juices uplift and balance the salty brine of the olives. It is a delicious and easy appetizer that looks elegant on any summery spread.

Preparation tip: These can be prepared several days in advance if stored and sealed properly.

Peel a few strips off the orange and grapefruit and set aside. In a small bowl or your transportation container, combine the olives, garlic, fresh herbs, and citrus juices, and mix together.

Add in peels, red pepper flakes, and drizzle it with olive oil. Give it a good stir or transfer to a plastic bag and toss it a few times. Let it sit in the fridge for 12 to 24 hours to let the flavors develop. Garnish with fresh citrus peels or herb sprigs. Serve the olives in a small bowl with some of the marinade.

FARRO & BROCCOLI RABE SALAD

Serves 4–6

1 cup farro

2 cups broth or water
   (I prefer chicken broth)

Extra virgin olive oil

1 15.5 oz can of garbanzo beans

¼ teaspoon red pepper flakes

1 shallot, minced

1 bunch broccoli rabe, stems trimmed

¼ cup water

2 garlic cloves, minced

1 lemon

1 tablespoon lemon zest

2 cups fresh basil, roughly torn

½ cup Parmigiano-Reggiano shavings

½ teaspoon kosher salt

Cracked black pepper to taste

This toasty and nutty salad is an ode to my love of broccoli rabe. Partnered with the ancient grain farro, is utterly delicious with roasted chickpeas and a zing of lemon.

Preparation tip: *If in a time pinch, cook the farro a day beforehand, keeping it in the fridge, and finish it off the day of your outing.*

In a small saucepan with a fitted lid, add the farro and 2 cups of stock and bring to a boil. Once it reaches a boil, cover and lower to a simmer. Cook until the grains are tender, about 12–15 minutes.

Fluff the grains with a fork and chill the farro in the fridge for about 30 minutes.

Meanwhile, in a small cast-iron skillet over medium heat, add 2 tablespoons of olive oil. Once the oil is warmed, add the garbanzo beans. Crisp the garbanzo beans over medium heat for about 10–12 minutes, stirring occasionally to toast evenly. Season with a pinch of kosher salt and the red pepper flakes. Transfer the garbanzo beans into a small bowl and set aside for now.

Remove the cooled farro from the fridge. In the same pan used to toast the garbanzo beans, over medium heat, add 2 tablespoons of olive oil. Once warmed, add the farro and toast for about 8–10 minutes until lightly crisp. Set aside.

In a large sauté pan, add 3 tablespoons of olive oil. Once warmed, add the shallots and cook until softened about 5 minutes. Add in the broccoli rabe and a ¼ cup of water. Cover and cook on low for about 10 minutes until tender, stirring occasionally. Stir in the minced garlic and set aside.

Combine the farro and broccoli rabe in a large serving bowl and season with kosher salt to taste. Squeeze in the juice of one lemon, lemon zest, and drizzle 2 tablespoons of olive oil over the salad.

Top off the salad with the crispy garbanzo beans, fresh basil, and Parmigiano-Reggiano shavings. Season with fresh cracked black pepper and additional red pepper flakes if you desire.

This salad is delicious served either hot or cold. It also can be made a day beforehand. Pack the salad in a leakproof container and serve in a wood or enamel bowl at your picnic site.

PAN BAGNAT

Serves 4

1 large ciabatta
   (or 2, depending on the size)
3–4 tablespoons salted butter,
   softened
½ cup pitted Castelvetrano olives,
   roughly chopped
½ cup pitted Kalamata olives, roughly
   chopped
1 tablespoon capers
½ cup roughly torn basil
½ cup Italian parsley, roughly chopped
1 garlic clove, minced
1 tablespoon extra virgin olive oil
Cracked black pepper
10 oz (2 tins) high-quality tuna packed
   in olive oil, preferably sustainably
   and pole caught
Juice of one lemon or 3 tablespoons of
   lemon juice
1 teaspoon kosher salt
1 small red onion, thinly sliced
1 heirloom tomato, thinly sliced
4–5 slices roasted red pepper

This is a Provençal picnic classic and certainly not one to be overlooked. What sets this sandwich above the average is its heft and sturdiness. While most sandwiches turn soggy and limp after some time, this one is preferable after letting it sit in advance for the ingredients to marinate together. It is certainly one to share with your fellow picnickers. There's no need to worry about crushing it either, as it's meant to be pressed by, say, a cooler or a happily obliging little one in the back seat.

Slice the ciabatta lengthwise into two halves. On each slice, spread butter along the nooks and crannies of the bread evenly. Set aside.

In a small mixing bowl, combine together the olives, capers, basil, parsley, garlic, and olive oil. Sprinkle on cracked black pepper to taste and let it stand for 10 minutes while you prepare.

Open the tuna and fork it out into a small bowl. Squeeze the lemon over the tuna, breaking it up with a fork.

Prepare to assemble the sandwich by laying out the two slices on a large cutting board. Spread the tuna mixture evenly over one slice of the bread. Sprinkle with kosher salt.

Spoon the olive and herb mixture over the tuna, gently spreading it over evenly.

Layer on the red onion slices, tomato slices, and roasted red pepper.

Gently press down on the sandwich with your hands.

Wrap the whole sandwich with plastic wrap or aluminum foil tightly. You can wrap butcher or kraft paper over the plastic wrap if you wish. It should be wrapped well to prevent leaking and falling apart on the journey.

While you are prepping the other picnic goods, place a heavy book or cast-iron pan on top of the sandwich. You can also pack the sandwich at the very bottom of your basket or cooler so it's weighted down.

Once you're ready to feast, cut it into 4 individual sandwiches.

STONE FRUIT GALETTE

Serves 6

For the pastry:

1½ cups all-purpose flour, plus more
for dusting

1 tablespoon granulated white sugar

1 teaspoon kosher salt

8 tablespoons unsalted butter
(1 stick), cold and cut into small
pieces

4–5 tablespoons ice water

For the filling:

2 pounds stone fruit (peaches, plums,
nectarines) cut into half-inch pieces
or quarter-inch slices

½ cup brown sugar

2 teaspoons fresh lemon juice

2 tablespoons all-purpose flour or
cornstarch

1½ teaspoon pure vanilla extract

¼ teaspoon kosher salt

2–3 tablespoons apricot jam

1 egg, lightly beaten

¼ cup turbinado sugar

Additional topping:

1 cup heavy cream (optional for
whipped cream)

1 tablespoon granulated white sugar
(optional for whipped cream)

1 vanilla bean, scraped (optional for
whipped cream)

A fruit galette is truly a picnicker's delight and best friend. It is also very adaptable to whatever ripe fruit you can find. Without the pressure of baking a perfect pie, the rough and ready presentation is the galette's true charm, making it an easy choice for a casual picnic with the family—or any occasion, for that matter.

Preparation tip: *Prepare the pastry a day or two in advance by storing it in plastic wrap in the fridge. Pull it out to assemble when you are ready to bake.*

Preheat the oven to 375°F. Prepare a parchment-lined baking sheet.

In a large mixing bowl, combine the flour, sugar, salt, and butter pieces. Using a pastry cutter, gently cut in the butter until it resembles coarse crumbs. You can also pulse them in a food processor briefly. Slowly add the water, and using a wooden spoon or your hands, bring all the ingredients together until it forms a rough dough.

Place the dough back into the bowl and let the dough chill in the freezer for 30 minutes.

Prepare the filling by combining the fruit, brown sugar, lemon juice, flour or cornstarch, vanilla extract, and salt, together until the fruit is coated.

Once the dough is chilled, roll out it out into a rough circle about twelve to fourteen inches in diameter and about a quarter-inch thick. Transfer the circle to the prepared baking sheet.

Lightly spread the apricot jam in the center of the dough, leaving three inches around the perimeter.

Add the fruit to the center of the dough, leaving a two- to three-inch border.

Gently fold the border edge over the fruit, leaving the center open. Tuck in any stray bits or patch up any areas with your fingers if need be.

Lastly, brush the crust with the beaten egg and sprinkle turbinado sugar on top.

Bake for about one hour, until the juices are bubbling and the crust is golden brown. You may need to tent it with aluminum foil to prevent it from browning too fast.

For the optional whipped cream, combine the heavy cream, sugar, and vanilla beans into a stand or hand mixer. Whip for about 3 to 5 minutes until it slightly firm but billowy. Serve with a dollop of the whipped cream on top once you are ready for something sweet.

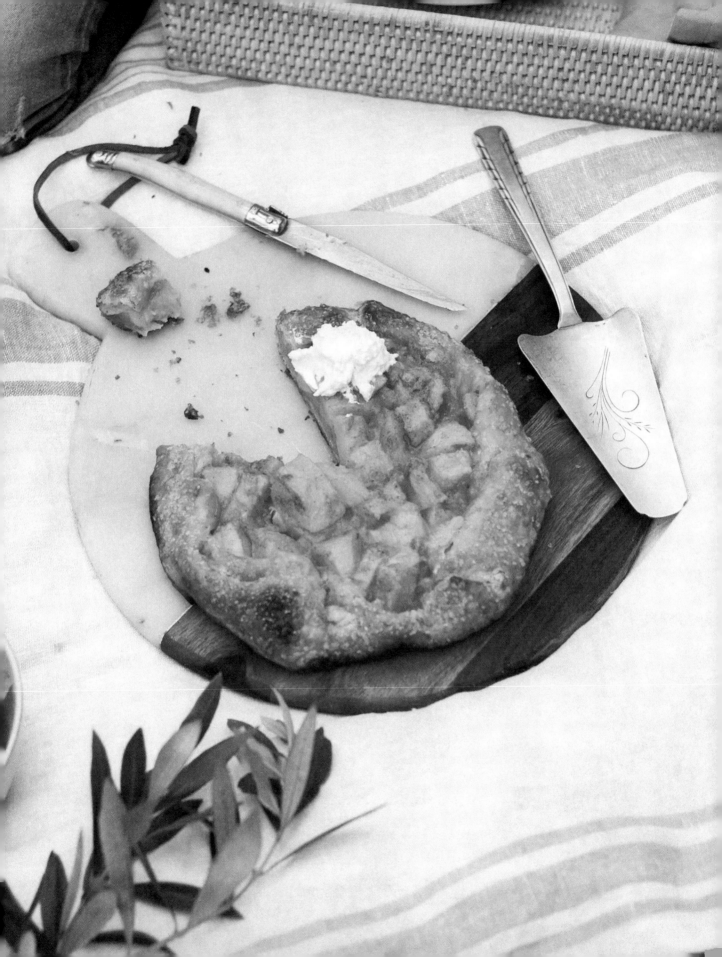

MAUKA TO MAKAI

Every August when I was young, we would pile in the car and drive several hours up to Maine. We would play a game to see which one of us could spot the blue ocean line on the horizon first by rolling down our windows, letting the strong seaweed and briny air fill the car. Passing lobster shacks and rows of classic New England white homes adorned with American flags, we finally arrived at our charming Victorian bed and breakfast. It was set behind an old stone wall driveway, just a short walk from the beach.

Once we got settled, we couldn't resist pulling on our swimsuits, packing our beach bags, and heading out the door. Popham Beach was our spot. The long boardwalks covering the sea grass led the way to a wide and powdery white beach. The days were filled with chasing seagulls, collecting shells, building castles and driftwood forts, and braving the brisk ocean. We packed light lunches with fresh fruit, sliced veggies, and sandwiches that were instantly devoured. In the evenings (with the exception of the picky eaters), we feasted on fresh lobster and seafood with copious amounts of butter. Our vacation always seemed to fly by and we dreaded the day when had to leave the ocean. Although when the time came to leave, with sandy feet and enough shells in our pockets to fill our bedside jars, we headed back home to the mountains. We savored every bit of that salty air that lingered on the drive until we reached inland.

I proudly consider myself a Vermonter at heart, yet the ocean has become a part of who I am. I can't help but be pulled by both the mountains and ocean simultaneously. They are entirely different experiences yet conjure the same feeling of peace and home. My hope for this menu is a true reflection and appreciation of both: something from the sea, the Earth, and little bit of aloha mixed in. If there ever was a time to let your hair down, feel the wind, and jump in the deep blue, summer is it. I truly believe that you can wash away any worry with a bit of saltwater, sand, and sun.

There is saying here in Hawaii to help orientate yourself on the islands: *mauka* (toward the mountains) or *makai* (toward the ocean). I feel like I'm somewhere right in the middle and I'm ok with that.

ROASTED CORN SALAD

Serves 6–8

6–8 ears sweet corn

4 tablespoons extra virgin olive oil

Juice of one lime or 4 tablespoons of
    lime juice

Zest of one lime

¼ teaspoon red pepper flakes

A dash cayenne pepper

1 teaspoon cumin powder

1 teaspoon kosher salt

½ red onion, thinly sliced

¼ teaspoon serrano chile, minced

2 cups cherry tomatoes, halved

4 cups fresh pineapple, diced

1½ cup chopped cilantro, about one
    bunch

2 garlic cloves, minced

1 cup unsalted whole pistachios

Cracked black pepper to taste

Summer corn is something to celebrate in any form, whether it rolled on top of a stick of butter or grilled as featured in this salad. I particularly love the toasty and nutty sweetness from the light char on the kernels which make a great pairing for those juicy summer tomatoes, too. You can serve it individually in Mason jars or transfer it into serving bowl at the beach. If you do use a bowl, be sure to cover it with a tea towel to keep out the sand and bugs.

There are two options to prepare the corn, grilling or roasting in the oven. Either way, the result is relatively the same, except grilling gives the corn a nice and crispy char which is delicious.

To grill the corn, prepare the grill on medium heat. If using a charcoal grill, make sure the coals are nice and hot and smoldering throughout, which takes about 30 minutes or so.

Gently fold back the husks and remove the silk threads. Lightly brush the ears with a little olive oil. Smooth the husks back down to cover the corn kernels.

Once the grill is ready, place the corn directly on the grill, turning every 5 minutes or so. Grill the ears for 15 minutes until the kernels are tender and no longer opaque. They also will be a brighter yellow. For extra char, fold back the husks and grill the corn directly on the heat for a few minutes, turning occasionally.

If you choose to roast the corn, preheat the oven to 400°F. Remove the husk and silk from the corn. Lightly brush the ears with a bit of olive oil. Set the ears right on the baking rack in the oven. Roast for about 20 to 25 minutes, turning occasionally to cook evenly. The kernels will be a brighter yellow and no longer opaque. For a bit of extra char, turn on the broiler for about 10 minutes and turn them once or twice until your desired amount of char.

Once the corn is cooked and fully cooled, using a serrated knife, remove the kernels by holding one end of the ear and slice down from top to bottom. Repeat with the remaining corn, cutting as close to the core as you can. Place all the kernels in a large bowl and set aside.

In another large bowl, whisk together the olive oil, lime juice, lime zest, red pepper flakes, cayenne pepper, cumin, and kosher salt.

Add the corn, red onions, serrano chile, cherry tomatoes, pineapple, cilantro, garlic, and pistachios to the lime dressing. Toss together until coated and season with fresh cracked pepper to taste and additional kosher salt if necessary.

GRILLED SHRIMP SKEWERS

Serves 6–8

For the shrimp:

½ cup whole fat coconut milk

Juice of one lime, about ¼ cup

2 garlic cloves, minced

1½ teaspoon of paprika

A dash cayenne pepper

1 cup cilantro, chopped

1 teaspoon kosher salt

1 pound uncooked and deveined
    shrimp, (frozen or fresh) 30–40
    count

2 cups fresh pineapple cut into one- to
    two-inch pieces

2 cups whole cherry tomatoes

Maldon salt

Cracked black pepper

For the herb dipping sauce:

3 cups firmly packed cilantro, stems
    removed (about 3 bunches)

½ cup fresh oregano

½ cup fresh Italian parsley, stems
    removed

2 garlic cloves

1 tablespoon white vinegar

¼ cup macadamia nuts

1½ cups extra virgin olive oil

1 teaspoon kosher salt

Cracked black pepper

These shrimp skewers are both satisfying and simple to prepare with just the right amount of tropical sweetness for wherever you may be. They also won't leave you feeling heavy while you paddle out.

Preparation tip: *Assemble the skewers and sauce the night before so you can pack up quickly and head out in the morning. Keep them wrapped in foil until serving to prevent blowing sand and forever hungry bugs away.*

If you are using bamboo skewers, soak the skewers in water for at least 30 minutes to prevent them from burning.

Preheat the grill to 450°F or medium-high heat. If you are using a charcoal grill, be sure that the coals are hot and smoldering which takes about 30 minutes.

Rinse the shrimp briefly in a colander over cool water and set aside.

To prepare the marinade, in a large bowl combine the coconut milk, lime juice, garlic, paprika, cayenne pepper, cilantro, and salt. Add in the shrimp and gently toss them together to coat them evenly in the marinade.

Let the shrimp rest in the marinade for at least a half hour in the fridge.

When you are ready to grill, begin to assemble the skewers by adding one shrimp, pineapple, and tomato continuing in that pattern until the skewer is full, leaving about a half-inch space between each piece. If you are going to grill at the beach, place the skewers into a gallon Ziplock bag to transport.

Place the skewers on the hot grill, turning once or twice, grilling for 2 to 3 minutes on each side. The shrimp should be bright pink and no longer a translucent gray.

Once they are all grilled, lightly sprinkle a dash of Maldon salt and cracked black pepper over them. Serve the skewers immediately with the dipping sauce.

Herb Dipping Sauce:

In a food processor, combine the cilantro, oregano, parsley, garlic, white vinegar, and macadamia nuts.

Pulse a few times while slowly pouring in the olive oil in a steady stream Scrape down the sides and continue to pulse until it is smooth. You can add more olive oil if needed. Season with salt and pepper to taste.

MAUI BARS

Serves 8

For the pastry:

1 ½ cup all-purpose flour

1 tablespoon granulated white sugar

1 teaspoon kosher salt

1 cup sweetened coconut flakes

1 egg yolk

8 tablespoons unsalted butter, cold
and cut into small pieces

½ cup ice-cold water, plus a few
tablespoons if needed

For the filling:

4 cups fresh and very ripe pineapple,
chopped into quarter-inch pieces

1 tablespoon lemon juice

1 teaspoon pure vanilla extract

2 tablespoons unsalted butter, softened
and cut into small pieces

1 cup brown sugar

½ teaspoon kosher salt

1 teaspoon cornstarch

For the topping:

1 cup old-fashioned oats

1 cup all-purpose flour

½ teaspoon ground ginger

1 cup unsweetened raw coconut flakes
(you can use sweet if you like)

½ cup macadamia nuts, chopped

3 tablespoons unsalted butter, cut into
small pieces

Pineapple and coconut are two quintessential summer flavors. These bars are a light and refreshing treat that are portable and easy to pack in the cooler for the beach. If you're daydreaming of the tropics, these are for you. Top with a dollop of vanilla or coconut ice cream if you are ever so tempted on a hot day.

Preparation tip: *These bars can be baked a day or two in advance of your beach outing and stored properly in the fridge. Keep them wrapped or stored until serving in the cooler.*

Preheat the oven to 375°F. Grease a nine-by-nine-inch baking tin.

In a medium sized mixing bowl, combine the flour, sugar, salt, and sweetened coconut flakes. Once thoroughly combined, add the egg yolk and butter pieces. Using a wooden spoon, stir together just until it becomes a shaggy dough. Using a pastry cutter, cut in the butter until it resembles pea-sized crumbs distributed throughout.

Pour the half cup of ice water into the bowl. Using your fingers or spoon, gently incorporate the water into the pastry. On a lightly floured work surface, turn out the pastry. It will be very crumbly. Without overworking it, sprinkle a tablespoon or two of the ice water if needed to bring it together with your hands to form a rough ball. Chill the dough for at least a half hour in the fridge.

You can also make the dough in a food processor, pulsing all the dry ingredients and butter together and then slowly adding the yolk and ice water until it just comes together into a flaky dough.

While the pastry is chilling, gather a small bowl for the filling and combine the pineapple, lemon juice, vanilla extract, butter, brown sugar, salt, and cornstarch. Using a wooden spoon, ensure the pineapple is covered evenly with the mixture. Set aside.

Pull the pastry out of the fridge to prepare the base. Using your fingers, pat it down at the base of the tin, covering all corners evenly. It should be about half an inch thick. Prick with a fork all around. Bake for 8 minutes until its pale gold and slightly damp with melted butter. Leave the oven on and set aside for now.

Prepare the crumb topping by combining the oats, flour, ginger, coconut flakes, and macadamia nuts. Work in the butter with your fingers until it resembles coarse crumbs throughout.

To assemble the bars, spoon the pineapple filling over the baked shortbread in the tin evenly. Sprinkle the crumb mixture over the pineapple filling.

Bake for another 20 to 25 minutes until the top is lightly golden and the pineapple is bubbling along the edges. If the coconut is browning too quickly, tent the bars with aluminum foil to finish.

Let the bars completely cool before cutting into them. They will cut much easier and cleaner. You can also stick the bars into the fridge or freezer if in a rush. They can also be frozen for up to 3 to 5 days.

WATERMELON & BASIL COOLER

Serves 4

5 cups seedless watermelon,
    cut into cubes

1 English cucumber, peeled and cubed

6–8 basil leaves

2 tablespoons wildflower honey

Juice of one lime

1 teaspoon lime zest

Optional: cucumber slices and basil to
    garnish

Watermelon, cucumber, and basil are the summer stars of this drink. Not only are they plentiful in the garden, they are refreshing on a hot day at the beach. It's not too sweet for something so pink! For a little extra sparkle, add sparking soda or champagne for bubbles.

In a blender, purée the watermelon, cucumber chunks, and basil leaves until smooth.

Pour the purée over a fine-mesh sieve set over large pitcher, using a rubber spatula to scrape and press down the remaining fibers.

Stir in the honey, lime juice, and lime zest until thoroughly combined.

Serve with ice in individual glasses or a pitcher. Garnish with optional cucumber slices and basil.

Transportation Tip *Store the drink in a large Mason jar or sealed pitcher in your cooler for transportation. Keep the garnishes in a separate smaller container. Don't forget the ice!*

A SUNDAY KIND OF LOVE

There are perhaps few things more synonymous with romance than a secluded picnic. Sharing a meal outside, even a humble loaf of bread and cheese, is quite intimate and endearing for two. However you paint it, picnicking is romantic, indeed.

When I studied abroad in Paris, I often found myself sitting on a bench munching away on a crusty baguette, watching the ever-fashionable Parisians going about their day. People often had lunch outside along the Seine midday. You could easily tell which ones were couples, a first meeting, or just friends. In reality, the city oozes romance and passion. A baguette, bottle of wine, and a seat for two under the twinkling lights of the Eiffel Tower et voilà! Romance.

As wistful and romantic as it may seem, a trip to Paris with a lover isn't the only place to create an intimate moment for two. The most charming and thoughtful gestures are sometimes the simplest. It's the quiet spot off the beaten track that holds meaning for me. The secluded corner of the beach that is rarely occupied or the quiet found in the woods is more like it. A great date, in my mind, is more about the intention and thoughtfulness behind it. I think that no matter what you bring along or where you go, what is more important is the attentiveness in the present moment. Planning a sweet outing for your partner is an opportunity for just that.

It doesn't have to be an elaborate affair. Packing a backpack full of delicious bites and setting out for a hike or grabbing a picnic blanket and a hamper of food to spread out in an outdoor space is all it really takes. A Friday night that may have been dinner and a movie can just as well be a picnic in the neighborhood park or sitting outside overlooking a beautiful view that's close to home. It really is that simple. Perhaps this is a picnic you can prepare together! The connection of truly seeing and listening to each other is what counts. I think we all could do with more of that in our lives, regardless of a relationship status. Plus, the view doesn't hurt either.

ROASTED POTATOES WITH ASIAGO

Serves 2

½ pound Yukon gold potatoes, washed
    and cut into quarters or sixths (I
    prefer unpeeled)
¼ cup extra virgin olive oil
1 teaspoon kosher salt
1 tablespoon unsalted butter, melted
1 cup asiago cheese, grated
1 teaspoon Italian seasoning (thyme,
    rosemary, and oregano)
Cracked black pepper to taste
Maldon salt to sprinkle

Rather than pairing grilled steak with classic fries, these crisp roasted potatoes are equally as tempting and healthier to boot. The savory addition of asiago cheese and herbs make these golden nuggets quite an addicting upgrade, if I say so myself. Without the heavy grease of traditional fries, they are a delectable accompaniment for a romantic evening for two.

Preheat the oven to 400°F and gather a small roasting pan.

Add the potatoes in a medium mixing bowl with the olive oil, salt, butter, asiago cheese, Italian seasoning, and a few turns of fresh cracked black pepper. Toss and coat the potatoes evenly.

Turn out the potatoes onto the roasting pan and roast for about 45 minutes, turning once or twice with a spatula until golden and crispy.

Season with a sprinkle of Maldon salt. Serve warm.

> **Transportation Tip** *To keep the potatoes warm, wrap them in a parcel of aluminum foil. You can also place the parcel right on the grill to reheat if needed.*

GRILLED STEAK & TANGERINE SALAD

Serves 2

Extra virgin olive oil

1 tablespoon whole coriander seeds

1 tablespoon black peppercorn

½ teaspoon red pepper flakes

¼ cup tangerine juice

2 garlic cloves, minced

½ cup cilantro, minced

½ cup Italian parsley, minced

1½ teaspoon kosher salt

1½ pounds New York strip steak

Pinch Maldon salt

6–8 leaves butter lettuce

½ cup radicchio, chopped

2–3 tangerines, peeled and cut into thin rounds

½ cup cherry tomatoes, halved

1 small red onion, thinly sliced into rings

Cilantro chopped to garnish

For the dressing:

2 tablespoons white wine vinegar

¼ cup tangerine juice or about one tangerine

1 shallot minced

½ teaspoon grainy mustard

1 teaspoon tangerine zest

¼ teaspoon kosher salt

¼ cracked black pepper

½ cup extra virgin olive oil

This salad is both substantial and light, special for a quiet evening overlooking the sunset. The fresh herbs and tangerines uplift the dish as grilled meat can often feel quite heavy for an intimate meal for two. With simple ingredients, it is an exceptional dish to serve for a special occasion or just to shake up the work week dynamic with a date night in the backyard.

In a cast-iron skillet over medium heat, add a tablespoon of extra virgin olive oil and toast the coriander seeds, black peppercorns, and red pepper flakes for 2 to 3 minutes until fragrant. Lightly swirl the spices together and remove from heat.

In a large gallon bag, add the tangerine juice, ¼ cup of extra virgin olive oil, garlic, cilantro, parsley, salt, and the toasted spices. Add the two steaks to the bag and seal it closed. Fully coat each with the marinade by gently turning the bag between both hands. Let it marinate at least 2 hours, or overnight ideally, in the fridge.

If you are cooking on a charcoal grill outside, begin to prepare the grill until you have smoldering hot coals, which takes about 45 minutes or so. If you are grilling inside or on a gas grill, you can simply start it up when you are ready to grill.

Begin to prepare the dressing in a small bowl by combining the white wine vinegar, tangerine juice, shallot, mustard, tangerine zest, kosher salt, and cracked black pepper. Whisk together until thoroughly incorporated. While whisking, slowly pour in the extra virgin olive oil until the dressing is emulsified. You can add more juice or vinegar, depending on your taste.

To assemble the salad, layer the butter lettuce leaves with chopped radicchio on each plate or in your transportation container. Slice the steak into thin strips place them on top of the bed of lettuce with the tangerine rounds, cherry tomatoes, and red onion rings. Garnish with chopped cilantro.

Transportation Tip *If you plan to grill at your picnic location, prep the salad beforehand in one container and add the steak with the dressing later. You can also prepare it all at home in one large container and divide it into two servings at your picnic.*

BURRATA WITH GRILLED PEACHES & HONEY

Serves 2

2–3 ripe peaches, halved with pits
    removed

Extra virgin olive oil

4 oz. burrata

Wildflower honey

Balsamic vinegar

Kosher salt

Optional: basil leaves, honeycomb, or
    chopped pistachios to garnish

There is something so luscious about a fresh burrata. Simply paired with ripe, juicy peaches and wildflower honey, it is as luxuriously delicious as it gets. It's a lighter alternative that I find just as decadent as any chocolate dessert. A little summer sweetness that feels as romantic as ever. If you can't find burrata, vanilla bean ice cream suits this recipe equally as well.

Depending on what type of grill you used with the previous steak recipe, light the grill over medium heat if gas, or if you used the charcoal method, grill the peaches last.

Brush the peach halves with olive oil.

Place the cut side down on to the grill for about 5 minutes. Leave them untouched for crisp grill marks.

Using tongs or a fork, flip the peaches over onto the soft skin side and grill for an additional 4 minutes or so. Once seared, remove from the grill and set aside.

Place the whole burrata round onto a single serving plate for two. Top with the grilled peaches and drizzle with honey, a splash of balsamic vinegar, and sprinkle of kosher salt. Garnish with additions and serve immediately to enjoy together.

ROSÉ 75

Serves 2

½ oz of Chambord

½ oz Hendricks Gin

2 drops rose water

Rosé Champagne, such as Veuve
    Clicquot Brut Rosé or the best you
    can afford

Dash of cracked pink peppercorns

Raspberries

Rose petals

Rose anything has my heart, especially the vintage English garden varieties and champagne, of course. This one is a twist on the classic and ever so elegant cocktail, the French 75. The pink peppercorns add a little spice which is always an essential for an evening for two. Who can resist the allure of champagne?

In each champagne flute, pour in the Chambord equally between both.

Using a bar spoon or the back of a spoon, slowly pour in the gin to create layers if you wish or pour in directly.

Add a drop of rose water to each flute. Top off each off with rosé champagne. Garnish each with cracked pink peppercorns, a raspberry, and one rose petal.

> **Transportation Tip** *Mix together the Chambord, gin, and rose water in a cocktail shaker or Mason jar before you head out for your rendezvous. Once you reach your secluded spot, top it off with the champagne. Keep the garnishes in a small separate container.*

STARGAZER SOIRÉE

One of the highlights of the summer is the meteor showers that spark in the dark sky of early August. The bright bursts streak across the night in what feels like the last hurrah of the summer season. Back home in Vermont, we are fortunate enough to have no light pollution and when the sun sets, the glow of the brilliant diamond-filled sky is slowly revealed. Not only did the Perseids meteor shower mark the end of summer, but the start of the school season. Knowing we would soon be back at our desks, we tried to squeeze every last drop of the sweet summer by laying out to watch the shooting stars under bundles of blankets. We huddled all together in the backyard with overflowing popcorn in tow to watch the spectacular show set against the inky Milky Way that majestically arched across the sky. We tried to count every one we saw by shouting aloud with each flash, especially with the dramatic and lingering ones that fell across our entire view. Not only was it one of our last summer soirées, it was a moment of stillness and awe for the dazzling spectacle in our own backyard that occurred only once a year.

That childlike wonder and awe that celestial summer skies ignited in me then still remains with me today, especially living in Hawaii. The Hawaiian Islands are one of the remotest places on Earth and have some of the clearest night skies for stargazing. Just beyond the backyard of my cottage is the grand crater Haleakalā, that rises up in big blue sky and is home to the island's observatory. The stillness and peace that stargazing brings for me is equally mixed with emotions of awe, curiosity, and self-reflection. No matter where you find yourself on this amazing-yet-fragile planet, when you look up on the starriest of nights you can't help but wonder if there has to be something greater. So, with that, gather your friends, candles, blankets, pillows, and these sweet and savory treats to experience the natural wonders that glitter and streak across the summer night.

Midnight Popcorn

Popcorn is one of those quintessential family treats for any fun evening indoors or out. I had to include two versions, one salty and one sweet, that are guaranteed to please everyone. Prep two big bowls as these will go fast; I would double each recipe for a family of four as it will sure to be gobbled up in the first half hour of counting shootings stars.

CACIO E PEPE POPCORN

Serves 4

3 teaspoons extra virgin olive oil

1/3 cup popcorn kernels

1 cup Pecorino Romano, grated

2 teaspoons whole black peppercorns

Maldon salt

In a large pot with fitted lid over medium heat, add the olive oil and popcorn kernels. Swirl the kernels around to coat them evenly in oil.

Let the kernels pop for about 3 to 5 minutes, slightly cracking the lid to release the steam. Cook and gently shake the pot until the kernels have all popped.

Grind the whole black peppercorns with a mortar and pestle until they are roughly ground.

Place the popcorn into a large bowl and lightly drizzle with extra virgin olive oil. Remove any unpopped kernels to prevent a cracked tooth! Add the Pecorino Romano and ground black pepper. Gently toss together and season with Maldon salt.

LIAM'S BACKROAD POPCORN

Serves 4

3 teaspoons sunflower or coconut oil

1/3 cup popcorn kernels

¾ cup maple syrup (experiment with
   infused maple syrups!)

4 tablespoons unsalted butter

1 teaspoon pure vanilla extract

Maldon salt

Optional: ground cinnamon

Preheat the oven 350°F. Prepare a parchment-lined baking sheet.

In a large pot with fitted lid over medium heat, add the olive oil and popcorn kernels. Swirl the kernels around to coat them evenly in oil.

Let the kernels pop for about 3 to 5 minutes, slightly cracking the lid to release the steam. Cook and gently shake the pot until the kernels have all popped. Pour out the popcorn onto the parchment-lined baking sheet into a pile.

In a small saucepan over medium heat, add the maple syrup and butter and bring to a boil. As the butter melts, constantly stir the mixture until it begins to bubble and foam, about 3 to 4 minutes. If you have a candy thermometer it should reach 240°F. Turn off the heat and stir in the vanilla extract.

Pour the maple syrup glaze onto the popcorn on the baking sheet. Use a rubber spatula to evenly coat all of the popcorn. Season with Maldon salt and cinnamon if you like.

Bake for 12 minutes, turning once, and then continue to bake for another 10 minutes. If you take a bite, the popcorn should be crispy throughout, not soggy.

Transfer to your serving bowl to cool. Sprinkle with additional salt to taste if necessary.

HERB ROASTED NUTS

Serves 6–8

3 cups unsalted raw mixed nuts

2 tablespoons extra virgin olive oil

2 teaspoons fresh rosemary, minced

2 teaspoon fresh thyme leaves

½ teaspoon orange zest

Kosher salt

These herb roasted nuts are a salty and savory kick for any night under the Milky Way. The orange zest adds a nice citrusy zing. Packed in a Mason jar, they make a great host gift or addition to a dinner party cheese board. Here's to a starry night party in the making!

Preparation tip: These can be roasted several days before your starry outing and stored in a tightly sealed jar for up to two weeks in a dark, cool place.

Preheat the oven to 350°F and gather a rimmed baking sheet.

Spread the nuts onto the baking sheet and roast for 10 minutes until lightly toasted and fragrant, turning once or twice.

Meanwhile, in a small mixing bowl, add in the olive oil, herbs, and orange zest and whisk together.

Remove the nuts after 10 minutes and toss them in the olive oil and herb mixture, coating them evenly.

Roast for an additional 3 minutes. Remove the nuts and generously season with kosher salt. Once cooled, transfer them into a sealed Mason jar.

COCONUT GALAXIES

Makes 6–8 bites

2 cups unsweetened coconut flakes
   or chips

1 teaspoon coconut oil

1 cup raw almonds

1½ cup dark chocolate chunks, 60–70
   percent cacao

1 teaspoon pure vanilla extract

Maldon salt

Of course, you need a little dark chocolate when counting shooting stars, how could you not? These coconut almond clusters remind me of swirling galaxies in the dark cosmos, topped with a healthy sprinkle of salt that resembles a splattering of stars. You can make them bite size for the little ones or larger if you are craving an indulgent treat. (Go on, it's dark, no one is watching!)

__Preparation tip:__ I like to make these a day beforehand to allow them to set in the fridge properly before settling in for a night under the cosmos.

Preheat the oven to 350°F and gather a rimmed baking sheet.

Prepare an additional baking sheet lined with parchment paper.

In a large skillet over medium heat, lightly toast the coconut chips until slightly golden, about 2 minutes. Be sure to constantly turn the coconut as it burns easily. Reserve a tablespoon of the toasted coconut chips for dusting on top.

In a small bowl, combine the coconut oil and raw almonds until they are thoroughly coated. Roast the almonds in the rimmed baking sheet for about 10 minutes until the nuts are lightly toasted. Once cooled, roughly chop the almonds into smaller chunks.

Meanwhile, prepare the melted chocolate by adding 4 to 5 cups of water to a small sauce pot and bring it to a boil. Place a glass mixing bowl with the chocolate chunks on top of the small sauce pot. The chocolate will melt slowly as the water below boils. Stir the chocolate occasionally to ensure all of the chocolate melts. Stir in the vanilla extract once the chocolate is melted.

Combine the roasted almonds and toasted coconut to the chocolate bowl until everything is thoroughly coated with melted chocolate.

Form a rough ball by spooning a tablespoon or two of the mixture on to the parchment paper.

Sprinkle with the reserved coconut chips and Maldon salt.

Let the rounds cool for at least one hour in the fridge to harden up before heading out under the stars.

AUTUMN

"AUTUMN IS A SECOND SPRING WHEN EVERY LEAF IS A FLOWER."

—ALBERT CAMUS

A DAY IN THE ORCHARD

In late September, when the trees become illuminated in gold and crimson hues and the air is as crisp as the leaves, apple season has officially arrived in Vermont. Buckets and crates are dusted off from the barn and lined up on the porch, empty and ready for our annual venture out to our favorite orchard. We have a few apple trees on our farm, but by no means do they compare to the bounty found at our local orchard just a few miles away.

Apple picking has been a family tradition ever since I can remember. Even the littlest among us would have the special duty to carry a small bucket down the rows. Spending a full day in the orchard does work up an appetite despite sampling an apple from every tree. We would pack a big basket with sandwiches to share, apple turnovers, and cider spread out on a wooly blanket, but the real treat was found at the orchard. Tucking into a bag of apple cider donuts was always something I looked forward to, fresh out of the fryer, still warm and moist filling the air with spices.

Last year, I flew back in autumn since I hadn't had a proper fall since I moved to Maui and I craved it desperately. I made a long list of all of the quintessential fall activities I could think of, tourists be damned. My family, anxious and excited for my return, planned out a day to visit a newfound orchard off the beaten track. Through nearly two hours of winding and narrow dirt backroads, we finally found it tucked away with just a plain and faded painted sign that you could easily drive past.

The old farmer came out of the wood cabin, muttering with a Vermont accent as thick as the woods behind us, and motioned to the carts nearby. My mother, who always has a spring in her step doing these sorts of things, hauled a cart away along the path. To what was initially a backwoods and rustic appearance eventually revealed an orchard unlike either of us had seen before. The trees were loaded with fruit, with branches barely able to withstand the weight, dripped to the ground. We kept exclaiming we've never seen anything like it as we filled our carts to the brim. The trees formed archways down the rows with apples tantalizingly hanging from above like burgundy, violet, and gold ornaments. As we left, we eyed the fresh cider donuts from the back kitchen and the farmer bagged up a dozen up for us. Plus, one more for good measure.

Images by Alanna O'Neil & Danielle Visco

ORCHARD HARVEST SALAD

Serves 4

For the salad:

1 bunch Tuscan kale (Lacinato or
    dinosaur kale)

1 bunch red kale, roughly chopped

2 cups radicchio, roughly chopped

2 McIntosh apples, thinly sliced

1 cup chopped pecans

½ cup raw pumpkin seeds

¼ cup pomegranate seeds

For the dressing:

2 tablespoons balsamic vinegar

2 tablespoons minced shallots

1 tablespoon grainy mustard

2 tablespoons maple syrup (Preferably
    Grade B)

3 tablespoons roasted walnut oil

¼ teaspoon kosher salt

Cracked black pepper to taste

When I think of the perfect autumnal salad, a bit of crunch, nuttiness, and a touch of sweetness ticks all the boxes for me. Tuscan kale is a hearty and forgiving green that only gets better with a little bit of rest, say, after a good walk through the orchard. It can be easily made in the morning before you venture out, leaving you not to worry about a soggy salad later. You can pack it up into individual Mason jars to serve easily.

Hold the stem of the Tuscan kale leaf in one hand and pull down along it with your other hand, removing the green leafy part. You can also cut the rib away from the stem if you'd rather use a knife. Chop the kale into one-inch pieces and set aside.

Prepare the dressing by whisking together the balsamic vinegar, shallots, mustard, and maple syrup in a large mixing bowl. Slowly pour in the roasted walnut oil and continue to whisk together until the dressing is emulsified. Season with kosher salt and cracked black pepper to taste.

Add the Tuscan kale, red kale, radicchio, apple slices, pecans, and pumpkin seeds to the mixing bowl. Gently toss the salad with the vinaigrette until fully coated. (The kale leaves will relax on your journey, so there is no need to massage them.) Sprinkle on the pomegranate seeds.

Note: *If you have the time to roast the nuts and seeds, all the better! On a baking sheet or cast-iron pan, gently toast the seeds in the oven with a teaspoon of olive oil at 350°F until fragrant and slightly crisp, about 8 to 10 minutes.*

MACOUN & BUTTERNUT SOUP

Serves 4–6

7 tablespoons unsalted butter

1 butternut squash, about 3 pounds cut
　　into one-inch cubes

3 carrots, cut into half-inch coins

3 stalks celery, diced

1 medium sweet onion, diced

3 fresh bay leaves

1½ teaspoon kosher salt

1 Macoun or honey crisp apple,
　　peeled and diced

1 tablespoon fresh thyme leaves

1 tablespoon fresh sage leaves,
　　roughly chopped

3 cups chicken broth or stock

½ cup half & half

Optional: chopped walnuts

When your hands are cold from picking the cool apples in the nippy fall weather, this soup with warm you right up inside and out. It is all the autumnal flavors of fall, pureed together for a smooth and comforting soup that can be easily poured into a thermos for day in the orchard. I prefer a crisp and bright apple for this soup, but don't let that stop you from using what you've got hanging on the branches outside or in your buckets!

Preparation tip: This soup is delicious prepped a day or two beforehand as it thickens with flavor. It also is a smart timesaving trick when you just want to head out and get to picking. It also can be stored in the freezer for up to two months and reheated on the day of your orchard outing.

In a Dutch oven or 8-quart stock pot, melt the butter over low-medium heat. Once melted, add the butternut squash, carrots, celery, onions, and fresh bay leaves. Sauté, stirring occasionally until the squash and carrots are softened and tender about 15 to 20 minutes. Season with salt.

Add the apple pieces and cook for another 8 minutes until softened when pierced with a knife.

Sprinkle in the fresh thyme and sage and stir until incorporated. Pour in the chicken stock and reduce to low. Remove the bay leaves.

Add the half & half, stirring until evenly blended.

Using an immersion hand blender, slowly blend the soup together in the Dutch oven until it is a smooth purée. A regular blender will do, too, just work in batches, pouring the purée back into the pot.

Season with fresh cracked black pepper and additional salt if necessary.

You can pack the soup in a large thermos and pour out into enamel mugs or bowls. For an extra special touch, sprinkle on a bit of fresh sage and chopped walnuts before serving. For any vegetarians, simply substitute the chicken stock with vegetable stock.

SWISS CHARD STUFFED BREAD

Serves 6

For the dough:

2¼ teaspoons active dry yeast

1¼ cups lukewarm water

1 tablespoon wildflower honey

3 cups bread flour

2 tablespoons extra virgin olive oil

1½ teaspoons kosher salt

For the filling:

2 tablespoons extra virgin olive oil

1 medium yellow onion, diced

1 bunch of rainbow Swiss chard
(2 cups cooked)

1 garlic glove, minced

1 teaspoon kosher salt

Cracked black pepper to taste

¼ pound prosciutto de Parma or
    soppressata

½ cup shredded hard cheese such as
    asiago or Parmigiano-Reggiano

½ cup fontina cheese, shredded

1 teaspoon dried oregano

1 teaspoon dried thyme

1 egg yolk

1 teaspoon water

½ cup sesame seeds

This bread is a savory delight all wrapped up in one with layers of Swiss chard, prosciutto, and melted cheese. On a brisk day, it's the perfect accompaniment for a hearty soup. It also is very forgiving, so if you have any last slices of ham or little bits of cheese hiding in your fridge you'd like to use up, layer them in.

Preparation tip: I'd bake this bread a day before you head out to the orchard. Although it is simple, it does take some time to assemble.

Using a stand mixer with a dough hook, on a low setting mix together the yeast, water, honey, bread flour, and olive oil for about 3 minutes until it becomes a sticky ball. Let it rest for 15 minutes.

Add the salt continue to mix the dough on medium speed until it comes together, about 8 minutes, scrapping down the sides if necessary. It should be satiny and elastic.

Transfer the dough to a lightly oiled medium sized bowl and cover with plastic wrap. Let it rise for 1½ to 2 hours until it has doubled in size in a warm place.

Meanwhile, prepare filling by trimming off the stems of the Swiss chard. If it is particularly a big stalk, remove the rib from the stems to avoid chunky bits in the bread. Cut the leaves into two-inch pieces and set aside.

In a medium sized sauté pan, add two tablespoons of olive oil and onions over low-medium heat. Sauté the onions for about 25 minutes until they begin to caramelize to a light brown color, stirring occasionally.

Add the Swiss chard and garlic to the pan, cooking the greens until wilted about 3 minutes. It should measure out to be about 2 cups. Save any extra greens if you like for later use. Season with salt and fresh black pepper to taste and set aside.

Preheat the oven to 375°F. Prepare a lightly oiled pizza stone or baking sheet lined with parchment paper.

Once the dough has doubled in size, lightly flour a work surface and turn out the dough, patting it out into an eighteen-by-eight-inch rectangle. Let it rest for 5 minutes, patting it further out if needed.

Spread the Swiss chard mixture onto the dough, leaving about a half-inch border around the edges.

Layer on the prosciutto and sprinkle the cheeses on top. Lastly, scatter on the dried oregano and thyme.

From the short eight-inch end, tightly roll the dough toward the other end gently. Once rolled, tuck in the two open seams under the bread, pinching the ends together.

Place the bread on to an oiled pizza stone or baking sheet lined with parchment paper. Cover with a tea towel and let the dough rise for another 45 minutes.

Meanwhile, prepare the egg wash by whisking together one egg yolk and a teaspoon of water in a small bowl until foamy.

After the second rise, brush the bread with the egg wash and sprinkle with sesame seeds.

Bake for 30 minutes or until it's golden brown. Let it rest for 30 minutes before serving.

MOM'S APPLE TURNOVERS

Makes 8–10 turnovers

For the dough:

2 ½ cups all-purpose flour

2 tablespoons granulated white sugar

1 ½ teaspoon kosher salt

6 tablespoons cold unsalted butter
shredded with a cheese grater

6 tablespoons lard

4–5 tablespoons ice water

For the filling:

4–5 apples such as Cortland,
Granny Smith, or Braeburn

1 tablespoon fresh lemon juice

1 ½ cups brown sugar

1 ½ teaspoons cinnamon

1 teaspoon pure vanilla extract

½ teaspoon kosher salt

2 tablespoons all-purpose flour or
cornstarch

1 cup half & half

Turbinado or maple sugar

Ever since I can remember, my mother made these apple turnovers come fall and winter. I think she did so partly because she felt that she could stick to eating just one rather than slicing little pieces of pie away throughout the day only for half of it to be gone. I love them because they are like individual presents all wrapped up in warm cinnamon, apples, and buttery pastry. It's also a wonderful way to use up any odd, spotty, or partially bruised apples you may have picked.

Preparation tip: Prepare the pastry a day or two in advance and store it well-wrapped in the fridge in plastic wrap. Bake them up the night before or morning of your apple excursion.

In a food processor, briefly pulse the flour, sugar, salt, butter, and lard until it resembles small, coarse breadcrumbs. Be sure not to over mix, make sure it still is very crumbly with bits of butter scattered throughout. Start by adding the ice water and gently pulse it as it combines together. It should hold together but still be rough and crumbly. If it's too sticky, add touch of flour. If it's too dry, add a tiny bit of ice water.

You can also make the dough by hand by combining the flour, sugar, and salt into a medium sized mixing bowl. Using a dough blender, cut in the butter and lard until it's in pea-sized pieces. Gradually add the ice water to bring to dough together into a rough ball.

Turn out the dough on a lightly floured work surface. Gently combine all the dough together to form a large ball. Place the dough ball back into the mixing bowl and refrigerate for at least an hour or overnight. The dough will keep in the fridge for several days.

Meanwhile, peel and core the apples. Cut into halves and then quarters for one-inch pieces or slices.

In a small bowl, combine the apples, lemon juice, brown sugar, cinnamon, vanilla extract, salt, and flour or cornstarch. Coat the apples evenly and set aside.

Line a baking sheet with parchment paper and preheat the oven to 350°F.

Once the dough is chilled, place the dough on the lightly floured work surface. Using a rolling pin, roll out the dough to form a large rectangle. It should be about a quarter-inch thick. Lightly dust the dough and rolling pin with flour as needed if it begins to get sticky.

Using a sharp knife or pizza cutter, cut about five-inch squares out of the dough. The bigger the square, the bigger the turnover. Cut out as many as you can and then reshape and roll out again to continue to use up the remaining dough.

Once you have a square, spoon a tablespoon or two of the apple mixture into one of the corners of the square. Gently fold over the other side to meet the apple-filled corner to form a rough triangle. Tuck in any little bits of apple if needed.

To seal, gently pinch the edges closed by using the pronged edge of a fork around the open edges.

Brush the tops with half & half and sprinkle with turbinado sugar.

Bake for 30 to 40 minutes or until the juices begin to slightly ooze out and become golden brown.

Serve warm or cold and reheat at 350°F for 10 minutes if necessary before your apple outing!

OLD-FASHIONED WASSAIL

Serves 4–6

6 allspice berries

1 teaspoon ground nutmeg

½ teaspoon ground ginger

½ teaspoon ground mace

½ teaspoon whole star anise

1 tangerine spiked with whole cloves

3 cinnamon sticks

6 cups apple cider

Cinnamon sticks to garnish

Whether bound for the orchard or not, spiced cider is a quintessential drink in our family during the chilly autumn months. Wassailing is an old tradition with a bit of revelry to ensure a good apple harvest for the year ahead. Our neighbors hold an apple harvest every October, pressing fresh cider by hand from the day's picking. If you aren't so inclined to press your own, this one will do for sure, especially if it's a local cider.

Add all of the ingredients to a medium sauce pot over medium heat. Bring it to a low simmer until warm, about 10 minutes. The longer the spices are warmed, the more flavorful the cider.

Remove the tangerine, cinnamon sticks, and serve immediately in a thermos. Serve hot and garnish with fresh cinnamon sticks.

THE MOUNTAINS ARE CALLING

The crisp and cool weather of the autumn is something I look forward to. There's a moment at the end of August that brings the ever so slight change in the air, hinting at cooler days ahead. The nights are colder, the daylight fading earlier with a brisk chill that makes you pull on one more layer. One of the true treasures at this time of year in Vermont is the spectacular and ever fleeting show that the trees put on once a year. Although I may be biased, the fall foliage in New England is one of the most beautiful in the world. The forests and mountains burst into flame in the sunlight in rich crimson, amber, and gold. I love to wander the woods to marvel at the colors before the wind or rain sweeps them away. Just as quickly as they come aflame, they turn to ash, brown and barren. I have yet to meet a Vermonter who takes this ephemeral moment for granted. I am a forever unabashed leaf peeper.

When I sat down to write this story, I recalled an amusing memory that stood out from the rest of my leaf peeping excursions. It was one of those postcard type of fall days, the leaves at peak color and the open sky a deep blue. We set out on an easy hike with a rewarding view at the top. Our big black bear of a Newfoundland, Reuben, came along, huffing and puffing the whole way. My mother, in true form, rather than packing a simple picnic, decided to bring a full roast chicken to make sandwiches when we reached the top. Our friend, Jane, insisted on carrying the backpack with our delicious provisions all the way up the trail. We were about halfway to the top when my mother pointed out that something was leaking from the backpack. We took a look in the backpack and found that the entire roast chicken was leaking and had soaked right through the backpack. My mother thought it was the most hilarious thing, unable to talk while trying to help wipe the chicken grease off of Jane who chided her for packing a whole roast chicken wrapped only in foil on a hike! Once we reached the top, we found that the grand chicken feast ended up a little battered but still delicious, despite the mess.

I will forever love to escape into the peace and quiet of the trees under their colorful canopy. After all, experiencing the magic of the foliage is best shared with company. Pack accordingly and perhaps leave the roast chicken for a cozy Sunday at home.

GOLDEN LEAVES SALAD

Serves 4–6

For the salad:

6–7 medium sized carrots

3–4 medium sized golden beets

1 cup red cabbage, finely sliced

1 honey crisp or golden delicious
apple, sliced into half-inch pieces

½ cup fresh Italian parsley, roughly
chopped

½ cup chopped walnuts

For the vinaigrette:

2½ tablespoons white wine vinegar

1 teaspoon wildflower honey

½ teaspoon kosher salt

½ cup extra virgin olive oil

Cracked black pepper to taste

Like the golden hues that set ablaze the Vermont mountains in the fall, this salad celebrates the vibrant colors of the season. The crispness of the carrots and apples pair deliciously with the earthiness of the golden beets. It tastes even better if prepared a day ahead of your outdoor adventure, allowing you to enjoy the moment for a fuss free day.

Using a food processor, julienne the carrots into roughly one-inch matchsticks, about 4 to 5 cups.

Peel and cut the beets into half-inch pieces. In a small pot with 3 cups of water, add the beets and bring to a boil. Cook the beets for about 10 minutes until tender when pierced with a fork. Drain and rinse with cold water and set them aside. Place them in the fridge to chill for a few minutes.

In a large bowl, whisk together the vinegar, honey, and salt. Slowly pour in the olive oil, whisking until the dressing becomes emulsified. Add the carrots, beets, red cabbage, apples, parsley, and walnuts. Mix and evenly coat the salad with the vinaigrette.

Pack up the salad in a large Mason jar or in individual small jars for each hiker to carry.

MANSFIELD PANINI

Serves 4

3–4 tablespoons unsalted butter at
   room temperature
1 loaf rustic sourdough bread, 6–8
   slices (depending on the number of
   people)
Grainy mustard
1 pound smoked maple ham slices
¾ pound sharp cheddar cheese slices,
   preferably Cabot
1 honey crisp apple, thinly sliced
1 tablespoon fresh thyme leaves
Fig preserves

A toasted sandwich to warm chilled fingers is sure to be appreciated on a brisk fall hike. The sharp cheddar, crisp apples, and smoked ham are a comforting autumnal trio when layered together. Opposed to a fresh sandwich, these panini pack thinly and easily into a backpack. You also won't have to worry about opening up a jostled and broken sandwich when you reach the top.

Heat a panini press or a medium cast-iron skillet over medium heat.

Lightly spread a pat of butter over one side of each slice. Spread a small dollop of grainy mustard over one side of a slice and lay flat.

Assemble the sandwiches by layering the ham, cheddar, apple slices, and fresh thyme on the mustard.

Top off the sandwich by adding a tablespoon of the fig preserves to a second slice of bread and close the sandwich.

Place the sandwiches, one at a time, into the panini press or skillet. Grill until the cheese is melted. If using a skillet, you can cover it with a lid.

Wrap the paninis in waxed paper or parchment paper. For extra security, tie with a kitchen twine or string, creating little individual parcels for each person.

VERMONT HERMIT BARS

Serves 8–10

3 cups all-purpose flour

½ teaspoon ground nutmeg

2 teaspoons ground cinnamon

2 teaspoons ground ginger

½ teaspoon ground cloves

¼ teaspoon mace

½ teaspoon ground black pepper

½ teaspoon kosher salt

2 teaspoons baking soda

8 tablespoons (1 stick) unsalted butter
at room temperature

1 cup dark brown sugar

½ cup dark black strap molasses

¼ cup hot brewed coffee

2 eggs

½ cup raisins

¼ cup crystallized ginger, cut into
quarter-inch pieces

¾ cup powdered sugar

5 tablespoons maple syrup, preferably
Vermont Grade B

Maple sugar (optional)

These are a New England classic. The lore is that sailors took these bars to sea because they lasted the journey until they returned, guided by the beacon of lighthouses along the coast. I find that the addition of hot coffee and crystallized ginger complement the warm spices and raisins nicely.

Preparation tip: *These bars can be baked several days in advance as they keep well.*

In a large mixing bowl, combine the flour, spices, salt, and baking soda and set aside.

Using a stand mixer with a paddle attachment, beat the butter and brown sugar on medium speed until creamy and smooth.

Add the molasses and hot coffee, slowly mixing on low so it doesn't splatter. Scrape the sides of the bowl and mix until combined. Crack one egg at a time, beating well after each addition.

Gradually add the flour and spice mixture, scraping down the sides of the bowl. Mix on low speed only for about a minute or two until it is thoroughly incorporated. Add the raisins and ginger, mixing until they are evenly distributed.

Remove the paddle attachment leaving the dough in the bowl. Chill in the fridge for one hour or overnight.

When you are ready to bake, preheat the oven to 350°F. On a lightly floured work surface, divide the dough in two equal portions.

Using a rolling pin or patting down with your hands, shape each portion into a ten-by-four-inch rough rectangle about a half-inch thick.

Place both logs onto a baking sheet lined with parchment paper, leaving about two inches in between each.

Bake for 12 to 15 minutes or until the edges are a light golden brown. They should be slightly underdone and soft rather than too brown.

Prepare the maple glaze by adding the powdered sugar and maple syrup into a small bowl and whisk together.

Glaze the bars when they are completely cool or else the glaze will melt off. Once cooled, using the whisk or spoon, lightly drizzle the logs on a wire cooling rack. Sprinkle on maple sugar if you wish.

Allow the icing to set before cutting the logs into individual bars.

PINNACLE HOT TODDY

Serves 4

3 cardamon pods

3 star anise

2 cinnamon sticks

5 whole cloves

6 cups water

2 tea bags PG tips or your favorite
    black tea

2 tablespoons Grade B Vermont
    maple syrup

2 ounces Irish or Scottish whiskey

2 lemon peels

Star anise to garnish

For those who need a little extra kick up the trail, this maple hot toddy will do just that. The aromatic spices pair beautifully with the maple syrup and whiskey that will warm you right through, too. You can, of course, leave out the whiskey if you like, either way it is a comforting drink while you rest on an old fallen tree. It also can be a rewarding drink to have after hiking while posted up by the fire for the remainder of the evening.

Add the cardamon pods, star anise, cinnamon sticks, and cloves to a muslin cloth bag or tea filter and place in a tea pot or thermos with the tea bags.

Boil 6 cups of water and pour into your carrier.

Add the maple syrup, whiskey, lemon peels, and a few star anise to garnish in your carrier.

You can make this into a large batch and then distribute into individual thermoses or one large one and pack a few enamel mugs to serve.

WINTER

"HE WHO MARVELS AT THE BEAUTY OF THE WORLD IN SUMMER WILL FIND EQUAL CAUSE FOR WONDER AND ADMIRATION IN WINTER."

—JOHN BURROUGHS

SNOWSHOE THROUGH THE WOODS

This picnic was inspired by my love for snowy days, but if you live somewhere milder, it can easily be adapted for a beautiful winter hike. Either way, in the dead of winter, when daylight is precious and the sun has a faint resemblance of its summer self, hanging low in the bleak sky, it takes a little willpower to venture out into the cold. Depending on where you live, the winter months can be anywhere from mild to a flurry of snow, to slush, ice, and more snow in every form imaginable. But even the snowiest of days can be perfect for a packed picnic. A backpack or small sled full of delicious goodies will make any walk through the woods an absolute delight. I've found that spending the day outside in the crisp air is always invigorating.

One of my favorite picnics for cold days with cloudless sunny skies and fresh snow is to pack a sled or backpack with some comforting treats and tramp down the trails in the woods with snowshoes. Horse and bike trails in the summer turn to snowshoe trails in the winter. When people say, "winter wonderland," it sounds horribly clichéd, but with fresh snow in a pine forest with golden sun rays filtering through the branches, it truly is. Everything glitters and sparkles. Nothing smells so fresh as a pine forest in winter when you've been cooped up at home for months.

Once everyone is good and hungry, it's time to stop to enjoy the feast. Snowshoeing or a brisk walk in the cold certainly works up not just a sweat but an appetite too! When I was a child, cups of warm soup, crusty bread, and cookies is what we usually packed for our family snowshoes through the woods. This picnic is a twist on those childhood favorites. The key is to keep it simple, warm, and hearty. Something hot and something sweet packed up on the sled with a wooly blanket is all it takes for a cozy snowy picnic. I have so many memories of winter feasts in the woods. It's only now that I appreciate those outings in the winter when I begrudgingly put on my snowshoes in the barn. I asked my mother why she always rallied us up to snowshoe when the more seemingly sensible idea was to stay inside. She told me her father did the same with her and her siblings every winter. It was he, she recalled, she owed her appreciation for the outdoors. Now years later, when I come home to visit for Christmas, packing up the sled for a winter picnic with my family in the woods is something I look forward to.

OLIVIA'S WINTER SOUP

Serves 8

3 tablespoons unsalted butter

1 medium yellow onion, diced

3 stalks celery, diced

2 garlic cloves, minced

2 15 oz cans of cannellini beans

8 cups vegetable stock or 2 32 oz
  packages

4 teaspoons fresh thyme leaves

3 teaspoons fresh rosemary, minced

2 teaspoon fresh sage, minced

½ teaspoon red pepper flakes

2 bay leaves

1½ teaspoon kosher salt

4 cups packed escarole, roughly
  chopped about 1 pound

1 Parmigiano-Reggiano rind

Cracked black pepper to taste

Parmigiano-Reggiano shavings

The winter season isn't complete in our house without one of my sister Olivia's hearty soups. She will find a humble bag of beans and suddenly whip them up into a comforting soup that is set out for the day on our old wood cookstove. Although she isn't as fond of snowshoeing as I am, this soup is my version that complements a wander in the deep woods.

Preparation tip: *If you make this soup on a cold winter night, it will last two to three days in the fridge. It also can be stored frozen in a large Mason jar if necessary and reheated.*

In a large Dutch oven, melt the butter over medium heat.

Once melted, add the onions, celery, and garlic and turn down the temperature to medium low.

Sauté the onions, celery, and garlic for 8 to 10 minutes, stirring occasionally. Reduce the temperature to low and continue to sauté for another 12 to 15 minutes until the onions are translucent and fragrant.

Add the beans, stock, thyme, rosemary, sage, red pepper flakes, bay leaves, and salt. Stir until well-combined. Continue to add the escarole and parmesan rind.

Bring to a low boil and cover with the lid for 5 to 8 minutes until the escarole is wilted.

Season with fresh cracked black pepper to taste. Serve with a generous topping of Parmigiano-Reggiano shavings.

WILLOUGHBY'S HAND PIES

Makes 10–12 hand pies

For the pastry:

2½ cup all-purpose flour

1½ teaspoon kosher salt

16 tablespoons (2 sticks) of unsalted
butter, cut into pieces and chilled

½ cup ice water + a few tablespoons
extra if necessary

1 egg yolk

1 teaspoon water

For the filling:

2 tablespoons extra virgin olive oil

1 medium onion, diced

2 garlic cloves, minced

1 small sweet potato, peeled and
diced in half-inch pieces, about
2 cups

½ pound Italian style mince sausage
meat

1 teaspoon fresh thyme leaves

1 teaspoon fresh rosemary, minced

½ teaspoon fresh sage, chopped

1 teaspoon kosher salt

¼ teaspoon red pepper flakes

Cracked black pepper to taste

Wrapped up like warm little parcels, these hand pies are very filling and quite simple to make as far as pastry goods go. They are quintessential picnic fare and for good reason, too. It can be an entire meal wrapped up in layers of flaky buttery crust which makes them all the more tempting. While marching through deep snow, I bet you will have an appetite for more than one.

Preparation tip: For time saving purposes as well as for the flakiest pastry, I'd prep the pastry dough a day or two in advance and keep it well-wrapped in plastic wrap in the fridge. You can pull it out and assemble when you're ready to head into the woods.

Preheat the oven to 350°F. Prepare a parchment-lined baking sheet.

For the pastry, combine the flour, salt, and butter in a medium sized mixing bowl. Using the pastry cutter, cut in the butter until it resembles small coarse, pea-size crumbs.

Slowly pour in the water just enough until the dough comes together with your fingers in the bowl. Take out the dough onto a floured work surface and gently bring it together with your hands until it forms a rough ball. Sprinkle a few tablespoons of water over the dough if you need to bring it together into a rough ball.

Place the dough back in the bowl and chill it in the fridge overnight or in the freezer for 30 minutes.

Meanwhile, begin to prepare the filling by heating a large skillet or sauté pan over medium-low heat with two tablespoons of olive oil. Add the onions and sauté for 10 to 12 minutes, stirring occasionally.

Add the garlic and cook for one minute until lightly brown. Continue to stir and add in the sweet potatoes, cooking for another 10 to 12 minutes until lightly crisp with brown edges. Set aside while you prepare the sausage filling.

Combine the sausage, thyme, rosemary, sage, salt, and red pepper flakes in a medium sized mixing bowl. Season with salt and fresh black pepper.

Remove the pastry from the freezer and roll out the dough onto a lightly floured work surface into a rough circle about a quarter-inch thick. Using a four- or six-inch diameter biscuit cutter, cut out as many circles as you can and then reroll the pastry out until you use up the remaining dough. Lightly flour the rolling pin and dough as needed to prevent it from sticking.

To fill each hand pie, scoop a tablespoon of filling into the center of one pastry circle. Take another cutout pastry circle and gently roll it out once more so it is slightly bigger than the bottom circle.

Place the larger circle on top to fully cover the filling. Gently press down with your fingers to seal around the edges. Finish sealing the circles together by crimping the edges all around with the prong end of a fork.

Place the sealed hand pies onto the parchment paper.

To finish, lightly whisk the egg yolk with the teaspoon of water in a small bowl. Using a pastry brush, lightly brush the top of each hand pie with the egg wash. Prick a fork into the top of each one to release steam and juices.

Bake for 30 to 35 minutes until the top is a rich golden color. Once baked, let the hand pies cool for an additional 15 minutes before serving.

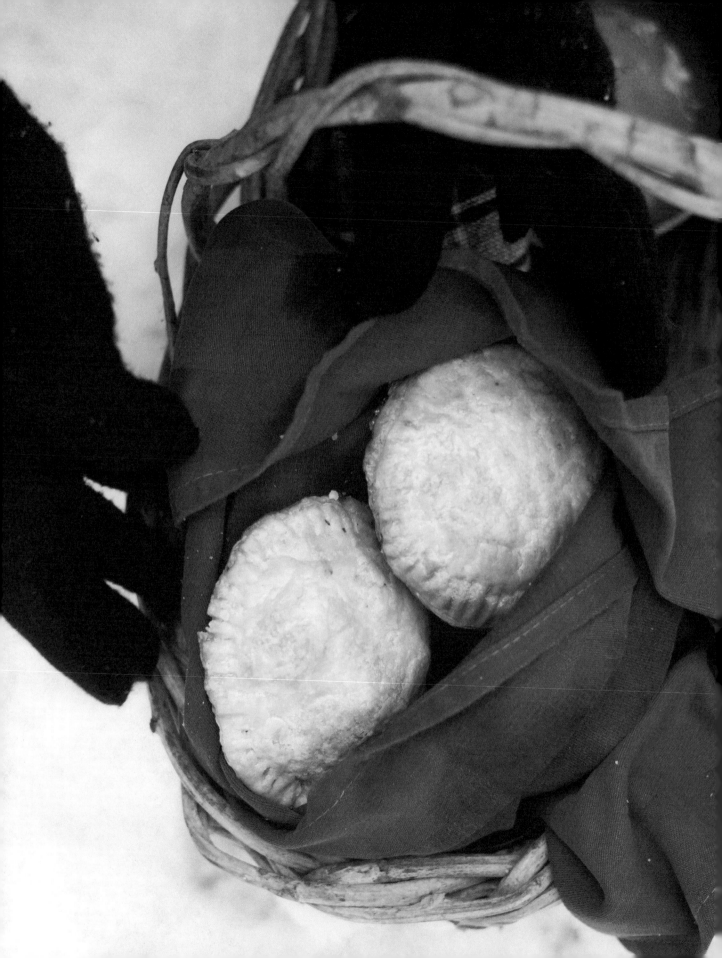

DECEMBER SPICED GINGERBREAD

Serves 6–8

¾ cup brown sugar

½ cup molasses

8 tablespoons (1 stick) of unsalted
    butter, melted

1 egg

1½ cup all-purpose flour

1 teaspoon ground cinnamon

¼ teaspoon ground nutmeg

½ teaspoon ground cloves

2 teaspoons ground ginger

¼ teaspoon allspice

½ teaspoon baking powder

¼ teaspoon kosher salt

½ cup hot black coffee

Powdered sugar for dusting

A winter picnic, or the entire season for that matter, wouldn't be complete without spiced gingerbread. Every year our family bakes some form of gingerbread, be it a cake or cut out cookies. For a snowshoe in the woods, these moist little cakes are quite substantial and bring some coziness while you take a rest under snow covered pine boughs. Even the squirrels may poke out to sneak a crumb.

Preparation tip: *These little cakes can be baked the night before and wrapped up and dusted with powdered sugar the next morning.*

Preheat the oven to 350°F. Grease 6 or 8 cup mini-Bundt pans with a nonstick spray. Add a touch of flour in each tin and lightly tap the flour around to fully coat every crevasse.

In a medium sized mixing bowl, whisk together the sugar, molasses, melted butter, and egg until it is a smooth and even consistency.

Add the flour, spices, baking powder, and salt and slowly stir together with a rubber spatula.

Pour in the hot coffee slowly while gently stirring together until the batter is a smooth and even consistency.

Fill each Bundt tin evenly, leaving a quarter-inch space from the brim of each tin. Gently smooth the top with the back of a spoon if necessary.

Bake for 20 minutes or until when an inserted toothpick comes out clean.

Let the cakes sit in the tins for 5 minutes before removing them on a wire rack to cool.

When the cakes are completely cool, lightly sprinkle powdered sugar on top.

Transportation Tip *The easiest way to pack these little cakes without crushing them is wrapping individually with parchment paper and kitchen twine. They can tuck right into a backpack for a spicy treat in the woods.*

SUGAR ON SNOW
HOT CHOCOLATE

Serves 4

4 cups whole milk

2 tablespoons 100 percent cocoa plus
more for dusting

2 oz semi-sweet chocolate, cut into
small pieces

1 cup heavy cream

½ teaspoon granulated white sugar

1 teaspoon pure vanilla extract

¼ cup dark amber maple syrup

Marshmallows

A warm cup of cocoa is one of winter's true delights, especially with rosy cheeks and cold fingers after a full day spent outside. During the sugaring season when it's a bit warmer, it's a New England tradition to pour fresh, hot amber syrup on snow which becomes a warm taffy. It makes a delicious and fun treat to top off fresh whipped cream over the cocoa.

Preparation tip: *Making the sugar on snow is by far the highlight of this recipe. You can make the maple snow before you head out or when you return, rosy cheeks and all.*

In a small saucepan over medium heat, warm the milk and cocoa. Whisk the milk and cocoa together until the cocoa is well blended.

Add the chocolate pieces in and whisk together until melted.

While the chocolate is melting, begin the whipped cream. You can use either a hand or stand mixer. Add the heavy cream, sugar, and vanilla extract to the mixing bowl. On high speed, whip for 8 to 10 minutes until it is billowy and creamy. Transfer it to a separate container and store in the fridge until you are ready to serve.

Once the chocolate is melted, keep it on simmer until you are ready to serve. Pour the hot chocolate into a thermos before trekking outside. To serve, top a mug of hot chocolate with whipped cream and a dusting of cocoa if you wish by packing a small snack bag of extra cocoa powder.

For a final festive garnish, in a small pot heat the maple syrup until it reaches 240°F on a candy thermometer. Immediately remove from the heat and slowly pour on a patch of clean snow outside or on a tray of gathered snow. Let the kids join in here; they will love it. Slowly pour the maple syrup over the snow and let it cool and harden until it's like taffy. You can keep the maple sugar snow in the freezer, too, as it will harden into shards that can top off the whipped cream.

A DAY ON THE HILL

Some of my treasured memories in the early winter were waking up to the first snowfall. Peering out behind the curtains only to see out of the frosted window a glorious surprise below was always a delight. The first snowfall blankets the farm with an ethereal stillness and peace. The sight feels like the warm recognition and familiar embrace of a loved one you've missed. The glistening snow and crisp air are invigorating and soul cleansing, snapping me wide awake.

The official arrival of winter heralded the start of our traditional sledding and skating parties. My mother used pull all three of us on our old wooden toboggan to the hill behind our horse pasture. We would spend the whole day out there until our cheeks were rosy, boots falling off and snow in our socks. But we didn't care; we were glowing with the thrill of it all, run after run. We would only come in to warm up quickly or bring out some hot muffins to the hill to warm our hands. Our neighbors put on annual sledding parties with lanterns and torches that lit the packed path to the hill making it look like a runway. We packed our sled with all sorts of comforting treats and a hot drink. When our mugs were empty and the chili pot scraped dry, we took our last few runs to top off a magical night and then followed the moonlit path back home to a blazing fire that awaited us. Winter outings can have just as much laughter, joy, and lightness with a delicious picnic, of course, as the warmer months of the year.

People always give me a curious look in Hawaii when I say we have winter picnics and parties outside in Vermont. I assure them that being properly dressed solves half of the problem but the truth is that Vermonters will find any excuse to be outside and know how to come prepared. Although, I love to cozy up to the fire with a good book and hot tea in winter, that hill in your backyard or the park around the corner is beckoning to you— whether it's snowy or not—to pack up a picnic to enjoy in the outdoors on a winter day. A hot thermos of chili and freshly baked cake will be sure to tempt even the most reluctant one in your company to come along!

CHIVE & CHEDDAR BISCUITS

Makes 8 biscuits

3 cups all-purpose flour

1 tablespoon baking powder

¼ teaspoon baking soda

1 teaspoon kosher salt

1 cup sharp cheddar cheese, grated

2 tablespoons fresh chives, minced

8 tablespoons (1 stick) unsalted
    butter, cold

1 cup cold buttermilk, plus a few
    tablespoons more

These flaky little biscuits are addictive; they will be gone faster than the first snow fall. Slathered with butter, these gold nuggets are delicious pairings for a hot chili or soup. They come together in just a few minutes and will be ready to pop into the sled in no time.

Preheat the oven 350°F. Prepare a parchment-lined baking sheet.

In a large bowl, sift together the flour, baking powder, baking soda, salt, grated cheddar, and chives.

Using a pastry cutter, cut the butter into the mixture until it resembles coarse crumbs. You can also use a food processor and add the butter, pulsing several times until it is a coarse mixture. Using a wooden spoon, gently stir in the buttermilk until the dough comes together into a rough mass. Chill the dough for 30 minutes in the fridge.

Place the dough on a lightly floured work surface and gently bring the dough together with your hands into a one-inch-thick rectangle. Be careful not to overwork the dough.

Using a three-inch diameter biscuit cutter or knife, cut out 8 biscuits and place them on to the baking sheet. You can of course cut them into any shape or size you prefer.

Bake for 15 to 20 minutes until they are lightly golden brown.

Once they are out of the oven, wrap them in aluminum foil under a tea bowl to keep them warm and tuck them away in your carrier.

CORIANDER CHILI

Serves 6–8

Extra virgin olive oil

2 medium sweet onions, diced

3 garlic cloves, minced

2 red bell peppers, diced

1 green bell pepper, diced

1 yellow pepper, diced

5 tablespoons jalapeños, minced

1 pound of roma tomatoes diced or
18 oz can

2 tablespoons tomato paste

1–2 pounds ground beef, 80 percent
lean

1 tablespoon ground cumin

2 tablespoons whole coriander seeds

1 tablespoon chili powder

1½ teaspoon kosher salt

1 15 oz can kidney beans*

1 15 oz can black beans*

2 ears of sweet corn, shucked and
kernels removed, about 2 cups

1 tablespoon white vinegar

Cracked black pepper to taste

Toppings:

1 cup green onions, chopped

2–3 chilies of your choice, chopped

1 cup sour cream

1 cup shredded extra sharp cheddar
cheese

½ cup cilantro, chopped

Avocado slices

When you have a full party, this comforting chili will be a crowd pleaser on a cold winter day. It's soul-warming, satisfying, and will warm your fingers, too! Everything seems to slow down in the winter and getting the family all dressed for a snowy outing can be an ordeal to say the least. Prepare the chili a day or two in advance to save some time when everyone can't seem to find their other mitten. To the hill we go!

If you want to use dry beans, soak 1 pound of each overnight by filing a large bowl with water until the beans are completely covered a few extra inches over the top of the beans. Cook them in the chili for an additional 30 to 40 minutes. For any vegetarians, simply omit the beef and double up on the beans.

In a large Dutch oven over medium to low heat, add a few tablespoons of olive oil. Add the onions and cook for 5 to 8 minutes until translucent.

Add the garlic and sauté for another minute or two until it becomes fragrant. Be careful not to let it burn as it cooks quickly.

Using a wooden spoon, transfer the onions and garlic to a small bowl and set aside.

Over medium heat, add a few tablespoons of olive oil to the same Dutch oven. Once warmed, add the peppers and jalapeños and sauté for about 8 minutes until they are softened, stirring frequently.

Add in the tomatoes and tomato paste. Stir in the ground beef, gently breaking up the chunks with the back of the spoon. Continue to cook until the beef is no longer pink. Season with the cumin, coriander seeds, chili powder, and salt.

Wash and drain the beans and stir them in along with the corn kernels and vinegar until the chili is well-combined. Simmer with the lid slightly ajar for an hour or so until it has thickened and reduced down a bit. Season with additional salt if necessary and cracked black pepper to taste.

Serve with your favorite toppings. You can keep these in separate Mason jars that are packed along, too.

Transportation Tip *If your sledding hill is off the beaten path, pack the chili in a screw top thermos or metal canister which is easy to carry in a bag or backpack. Serve in enamel bowls which help retain the heat and are also quick to clean up. If you are heading out in your backyard or not traveling too far for your sledding adventure; once the Dutch oven has cooled slightly, wrap and tie a dish towel or tablecloth around the whole pot. It makes it easy to hold and handle while carrying it on your sled or in your car.*

SPICED WALNUT RUM CAKE

Serves 8

For the cake:

2½ cups all-purpose flour plus a few
    tablespoons extra

2 teaspoons baking powder

1 teaspoon baking soda

½ teaspoon kosher salt

1 teaspoon ground cinnamon

1 teaspoon ground ginger

½ teaspoon ground cloves

½ teaspoons allspice

16 tablespoons unsalted butter, room
    temperature

1 cup brown sugar

½ cup wildflower honey

2 eggs

1 cup buttermilk

1 cup chopped walnuts

Grated zest of 1 lemon, about ½ cup[3]

Grated zest of 2 oranges, about ½
    cup[4]

Powdered sugar for dusting

For the glaze:

3 tablespoons lemon juice

½ cup fresh orange juice

½ cup brown sugar

½ cup wildflower honey

2 tablespoons orange zest

6 tablespoons dark rum

The nutty, sweet, and citrusy crumb is enhanced by the subtle hint of rum. Walnuts and citrus are a happy pairing in the winter months. Adjust as you see fit or simply omit the rum all together if you have any young ones coming along. It is also a wonderful accompaniment to a morning cup of coffee while watching the snow fall quietly outside. It is also sturdy enough to be transported for a snowy outing on a mild winter day.

Preparation tip: This cake holds its own if you bake it the night before your sledding party, allowing the rum to truly set in.

Preheat the oven to 350°F. Using a nonstick cooking spray or butter, thoroughly grease a Bundt pan. Add two tablespoons of flour to the greased pan and tap it as you rotate it in your hand, coating the whole interior. This is an additional step to prevent the cake from sticking. Continue to turn the pan in a circle and discard any remaining flour.

In a mixing bowl, sift together the flour, baking powder, baking soda, salt, cinnamon, ginger, cloves, and allspice. Set aside.

Using an electric mixer or stand mixer with paddle attachment, beat the butter on medium speed until it softens. Add in the sugar and honey and continue to beat the butter until it is creamy with an even consistency.

Add the eggs one at a time, beating well after each addition. On low speed, alternate adding the dry ingredients and buttermilk. Scrape the sides with a rubber spatula to ensure everything is well-combined.

Remove the bowl from the mixer stand and gently fold in the walnuts and citrus zests.

Pour the batter into the prepared pan and smooth the top with the back of a spoon.

Bake for 50 to 60 minutes until the top springs back quickly or when an inserted toothpick comes out clean.

Meanwhile, begin to prepare the glaze. Add the citrus juices, sugar, honey, and zest in a small saucepan over high heat. Stir the ingredients until the sugar has completely dissolved. Remove from the heat and pour in the rum. For any little ones about, simply omit the rum.

With the cake still remaining in the pan, use a fork or skewer to pierce the top of the cake (which will eventually be the bottom) several times around for the glaze to seep through. Pour the glaze slowly and evenly over the cake, pausing a few times to let it fully absorb. It will soak up every last drop eventually!

» 3   *reserve the juice for the glaze*
» 4   *reserve the juice for the glaze*

Once finished, let the cake sit for a few minutes still in the pan to allow the glaze to settle in. To remove the cake, cover the pan with a large plate. Holding the plate and pan firmly together, flip the cake over and it should gently transfer to the plate. If the cake does not come out as easy, lightly tap it with a knife until it breaks free.

When the cake is completely cooled, dust with a generous amount of powdered sugar. Serve in thick slices.

Transportation Tip *With colder temperatures naturally comes cold fingers. If it is a sunny and warmer winter day (by that, I mean 40 degrees), you can use a cake carrier for a backyard sledding outing. For a wintery walk, precut several slices and wrap them individually in a backpack.*

MULLED WINE WITH POMEGRANATES

Serves 6–8

3 tangerines

2 tablespoons whole cloves

750 ml (1 bottle) of full-bodied red
  wine, such as a cabernet sauvignon
  or merlot

¼ cup wildflower honey

2 cups apple cider

½ cup cranberries

1 cup golden raisins

1 cup raisins

1 teaspoon freshly grated ginger

5 star anise

2 cinnamon sticks + a few more to
  garnish

2 oranges, sliced into rounds

1 cup pomegranate seeds

Infused with cinnamon, cloves, and orange, this traditional winter drink celebrates all of the seasonal flavors. It's a classic recipe that will warm you through and through, especially with the wine-soaked raisins. Pomegranate seeds and cranberries add a festive touch that resemble ruby red gems in your mug. What's a sledding party without a little mulled wine?

Note: *Simply substitute the wine for cider to make this kid friendly; they will love the warm cinnamon. It also can be prepared two days in advance and kept in the fridge and reheated. You can also use a cheese cloth to hold all the spices and discard it when you're ready to serve.*

Pierce the tangerines with the cloves so that they are spiked all around.

In a large pot, Dutch oven, or slower cooker, pour in the wine, honey, cider, cranberries, raisins, spices, and orange rounds. Bring to a very low simmer and cook for 15 minutes or else you will burn off the alcohol.

Strain the liquid and transfer into a thermos or keep it in a slow cooker. When you are ready to serve, garnish with the pomegranate seeds and cinnamon sticks.

Transportation Tip *A large thermos works perfectly well as you can divide and share as you like. It's light and packable so that when your sledding party needs a hot drink to warm up, they can ladle the wine into enamel mugs for a toast or comforting drink. It can also be made a few hours ahead or chilled for 2 days. And of course, it is equally delicious enjoyed by the wood stove if the weather is appallingly bitter cold.*

THE PARTING GLASS

With many more joyous memories to create and share, I hope this book has been a bit of inspiration to gather in good company in the great outdoors. Each and every outing is as unique as the last. I can only hope you, too, will honor your own seasonal traditions as well as adopt a few new ones. May you cherish the little moments as well as the grander occasions, being ever present with an open ear and heart. Whether it's the towering mountains, pristine beaches, or simply your own backyard, having reverence for the natural world is just as important as wholesome food for our wellbeing and happiness. Our one true escape, a place to laugh, love, and wonder in pure awe at beauty surrounding us. Perhaps we will leave not only having a deeper understanding and respect for each other, but ourselves, too. Like good food, beautiful moments in nature are often best when shared. A heaping basket spread out in a quiet field with loved ones against the setting sun is a true gift indeed. Here's to good food, good company, and the great outdoors!

ACKNOWLEDGEMENTS

There are a few who I am forever indebted to in the creation of this book, namely my supportive and hardworking parents. The seeds of this book were planted long ago in my early childhood, and for that, I am especially grateful. Although my childhood was no near perfect, I've realized how it has shaped who I've become today. Their dedication and sacrifice throughout the years provided me the means and courage to follow my dreams. I owe my creativity to my mother and my discipline to my father, each enabling me to create this book. My mother especially has been my sounding board throughout the whole process, listening to me ramble over the phone from thousands of miles away, sharing her artistic perspective, and assisting me with styling in the frozen winter. Your feedback and creative eye are most valued of all.

My siblings, Olivia and Liam, are owed many thanks for their help and support on shoots, albeit begrudgingly sometimes. You both have provided constant support and feedback throughout the whole process, and I thank you for that.

A special thank you to my agent Jessica Alvarez who believed in me and this book from the start. I can't thank you enough for taking a chance on me with all of your support and guidance.

Of course, a warm thanks to Lisa McGuinness at Mango Publishing who also believed in this book from the start.

To the many friends who have added bits here and there, all of you have been wonderfully supportive. Richela, Gio, Austin, Emma, Elizabeth, Anne, Tracy, and others who have been involved along the process, thank you for all of your love, support, and encouragement.

ABOUT THE AUTHOR

Alanna O'Neil is a professional photographer, designer, and home cook. She has a degree in Global Studies and Fashion Design from Parsons School of Design. Her work celebrates visual storytelling and seasonal living. Originally from the Green Mountains of Vermont, she found a slow and peaceful bit of paradise in Maui to call home with her sweet puppy Winslow.

Alanna's passion for photography and narrative storytelling emerged from her background in fashion design. She worked in the high fashion industry in New York City before returning to her roots in Vermont and then creating a new life in Hawaii. Her travels abroad in Europe greatly influenced the concept of *The Art of Picnics*. She works regularly as a creative and lifestyle photographer for various food brands and magazines in the US and Europe.

This is her first book.

yellow pear  press

Yellow Pear Press, established in 2015, publishes inspiring, charming, clever, distinctive, playful, imaginative, beautifully designed lifestyle books, cookbooks, literary fiction, notecards, and journals with a certain joie de vivre in both content and style. Yellow Pear Press books have been honored by the Independent Publisher Book (IPPY) Awards, National Indie Excellence Awards, Independent Press Awards, and International Book Awards. Reviews of our titles have appeared in Kirkus Reviews, Foreword Reviews, Booklist, Midwest Book Review, San Francisco Chronicle, and New York Journal of Books, among others. Yellow Pear Press joined forces with Mango Publishing in 2020, both with the vision to continue publishing clever and innovative books. The fact that they're both named after fruit is a total coincidence.

We love hearing from our readers, so please stay in touch with us and follow us at:

Facebook: Mango Publishing
Twitter: @MangoPublishing
Instagram: @MangoPublishing
LinkedIn: Mango Publishing
Pinterest: Mango Publishing
Newsletter: mangopublishinggroup.com/newsletter